RICHTER ET DAHL ROCHA

CONTEMPORARY
WORLD
ARCHITECTS

RICHTER ET DAHL ROCHA

Foreword by
Jorge Francisco Liernur

Introduction by
Jacques Gubler

Concept and Design by
Lucas H. Guerra
Oscar Riera Ojeda

ROCKPORT PUBLISHERS
GLOUCESTER, MASSACHUSETTS

First published in the United States of America by:
Rockport Publishers, Inc.
33 Commercial Street
Gloucester, Massachusetts 01930
Telephone: 978-282-9590
Fax: 978-283-2742

Distributed to the book trade and art trade in the United States of America by
North Light Books, an imprint of F & W Publications
1504 Dana Avenue
Cincinnati, Ohio 45207
Telephone: 513-531-2222

Other distribution by Rockport Publishers, Inc.

ISBN 1-56496-451-5
10 9 8 7 6 5 4 3 2 1
Manufactured in China.

Cover photograph: EOS Headquarters by Yves André
Pages 1–3 photograph: Golay Buchel Headquarters by Yves André
Page 155 photograph: Pierre Boss Photographe
Back flap photograph: Yves André
Back cover photographs: Train Maintenance Building and Espacité, both images by Yves André

Graphic Design: Lucas H. Guerra/Oscar Riera Ojeda
Layout: Oscar Riera Ojeda
Composition: Hunha Lee

CONTENTS

Foreword

BY JORGE FRANCISCO LIERNUR

One of the most indisputable characteristics of contemporary Argentine architecture is the loss of creative tension. With few exceptions, and in most cases attributable to the almost militant desire of some creators, the majority of works (and projects) produced in recent years have a circumspect appearance, harsh in some ways, as though more skills than wisdom or passion had intervened in their conception. This condition has many causes, many of them related to the terrible events our country has gone through these last decades. This is obviously not the place to analyze them, but we could say that this lack of tension is the result of a triple act of simplification: first, by reducing a vast body of human knowledge and experience to a significant but only partial aspect of that body that is the project technique; second, by considering it first and foremost a professional praxis—when carried to an extreme, valued according to volume—rather than a discipline, a way of seeing and understanding the world, a cultural and therefore critical activity; and third, by assigning an exclusively evaluative role to what actually constitutes only one of the forms of project organization, that which attempts to obtain its unity through the paradigm referred to in academic theory as parti, known to us as "partido."

The result of this triple reduction is usually work praised for its "clear geometry," which confuses simplism with minimalism, in which the constructive aspect constitutes a secondary moment, added to the original "idea," and where the absence of time—that time for reflection proposed by Alberti and Mies—reveals an unconditional surrendering to the haste imposed by the marketplace. This "terribilità" has obliged numerous architects to leave the country, some of them having contributed in notable fashion to the international debate. Nevertheless the structure of contemporary culture's "North Atlantic–centricity" dissolves their origins when the movement is from the periphery towards the center, but not when in the opposite direction. In other words: The Tokyo Forum is not architecture from the River Plate in Japan, whilst the "Banca del Lavoro" in Buenos Aires is Swiss Italian architecture in Argentina.

For various reasons Richter and Dahl Rocha's work is provocative in the debate on this asymmetry, and it simultaneously constitutes a solid contribution to a debate of a more basic nature, at once local and universal. And for this reason this book is a fortunate step. On the level of an international debate their work can be said to be in the place of the "same," and here resides its provocative capacity: the most disturbing image of an assassin is the one of our innocent neighbor on the Metro, so close by. Richter and Dahl Rocha's path is not the explicit one of militant "vanguardism," therefore not disturbing to the majority—but rather of insertion in one of the most conservative societies in the world. The question running throughout the work of Richter and Dahl Rocha is one of creative margins within that model, of the possibility of introducing originality where there is greatest demand in the opposite direction. Their work does not perplex visually with presumably rotund affirmations but is rather a rigorous experience in subtleties. The interesting thing about their work is that, while on one hand they appear to border on banality, on the other they resist being reduced to an initial moment, to an excluding determination.

The coincidence is impressive. The paths of Richter and Dahl Rocha crossed in New Haven as students at the school that houses the legacy of Louis Kahn. What could a young man coming from the turbulence and darkness of Argentina in the seventies have in common with another brought up in the safe and opulent surroundings of the confederation in the Alps? My impression is that different roads led them to the place of sensible moderation that they share in their work today.

In Richter's case I believe there are objective, structural reasons for such moderation. Construction in Switzerland is strongly conditioned by strict regulations, by the democratic and decisive participation of its citizens in matters of urban interest, by the high technological level of constructive processes. In this context, and especially when working for large corporations, creative margins are reduced to a minimum, commonly allowed to disappear altogether. Clearly these "hard" reasons are not new, but they have given direction to a special cultural tradition for some time now. The so-called "modern Swiss tradition", that which emerged particularly following the publication of *La Nouvelle Architecture* compiled by Alfred Roth in the late thirties, represents a sort of "responsible" modernism, a credible, pacified response to the sustainability of new architectural forms within the Confederation's stable social and economic framework. With its care for constructive quality, material, workmanship, its rational functional organization, its elegant aesthetic manipulation, the "modern Swiss tradition" expresses a manifest rejection of simplistic regionalism, but above all, of the stridencies, the "pamphletism," and the excessive plasticism of other European modernisms.

I believe, however, that there are different reasons for Dahl Rocha's moderation. To a large extent, it is also the consequence of his own modern tradition. By this I mean the tradition of self-containment and discretion of Argentine architecture, which includes the work of Alberto Prebisch and Antonio Vilar, and which has matured recently in the work of Ernesto Katzenstein and Horacio Baliero. That tradition is part of an important current in Argentine culture that has constructed a minimalist paradigm on the practical and metaphysical impositions of the gigantic plain. For this tradition the radicality of Amancio Williams' work constitutes an excess. Dahl Rocha's "objective" motives are very different. While Swiss moderation is an adaptation to the dictates of an extremely solid socio-economic structure, Argentine moderation is a response to the absence of any stable point of reference. Dahl Rocha's moderation in his best works in Argentina is a choice, or rather a selection, of severe self-discipline as a recourse against the possibility of dissolution.

Golay Buchel Headquarters, Lausanne, Switzerland, 1997 (above).

The pilgrimage of that sobriety from the plains of Argentina to the Swiss Alps may seem surprising, but the coincidence is not rare. As many will remember, Jorge Luis Borges decided to live out his final days in Switzerland. On the other hand, the strange sensation of seeing the same image duplicated by different mirrors has antecedents that copy it. By the late forties the story of Richter and Dahl Rocha had already been told in a similar way with other names: the Swiss, Max Bill and the Argentine, Tomas

Maldonado. In that case also, simultaneously and for similar reasons, the two men found themselves postulating the same handful of ideas. Unlike Richter-Dahl Rocha, however, Bill-Maldonado believed in a total solution.

But it would be a mistake to assume that the architecture of Richter and Dahl Rocha is nothing more than craft and sobriety. The interest resides in the fact that it is precisely with craft and sobriety, with moderation and professional rigor, that they are able to construct imaginative and poetic architecture where originality is savored without anxiety. It is that imagination and that poetry that give way to an open, uncertain, and latent universe of meanings. The work of Richter-Dahl Rocha is perceived as complete precisely because it is capable of raising doubts about the certainties of the profession, because once these are reached they are surpassed.

It is true that despite clearly identifiable traits, this work is the reflection of a process of maturation. Perhaps one could ask them to take greater risks in some operations, to avoid the temptation of the contemporary or to practice greater economy of their own skills. I believe, however, that their work, even in its relatively early stages—we are talking about a period of only six years— proposes some important affirmations: first, that it is not inevitable that discipline be dissolved in the profession; second, that it is likewise not inevitable that projects be reduced to exercises in geometry; third, that research is possible simultaneously with insertion in the market; fourth, that the condition of materiality is a starting point that can become decisive; and finally that architecture, wherever it may be, is still capable of raising the same questions as ever, about great and small, space and material, beauty and utility, permanent and ephemeral, nature and society.

Sketch for a house in San Isidro, Argentina, 1988 (top); forest refuge in the Jura Mountains Forest, Switzerland, 1995 (bottom and opposite page).

Introduction

BY JACQUES GUBLER

CONTRASTS AND SURPRISES

A SHORT BIOGRAPHICAL NOTE

Jacques Richter, born in 1954, a Swiss lover of tango, and Ignacio Dahl Rocha, born in 1956, Latin American and an acute and critically nostalgic observer of European architecture, met and fraternized at Yale in New Haven at the beginning of the eighties. Richter studied at the ETH in Zurich and Dahl Rocha at the FADU in Buenos Aires. The many didactic stimuli experienced at Yale with James Stirling and Cesar Pelli or the repeated visits to Louis Kahn's Mellon Center for British Art offered a solid ground for their developing friendship.

Richter went back to his home city, Lausanne, on Lake Geneva, and worked in his father's office. Dahl Rocha returned to his home metropolis, Buenos Aires, on the Rio de la Plata, teaming up with Billoch and Ramos. Their "House in San Isidro" was shown in 1988 in Vicenza, selected for the Palladio Prize, and in the Buenos Aires Bienalle a year later. In 1987 Richter won the competition for the "Place Sans Nom" (Square without a Name) organized by the city of La Chaux-de-Fonds to celebrate Le Corbusier's Centennial. The open program was formulated as the need for a "courageous" urban proposal, the fostering of a new landmark in the heart of Jeanneret's birth place. To make a long story short, let us add that Richter and Dahl Rocha eventually succeeded in creating their own firm and partnership. Being the successors of Richter's father's confirmed practice was no doubt helpful, but they had proved their independence by winning prizes and competitions that would allow them to be themselves and develop their own "themes in architecture."

CAN A SINGLE BOX BE ARTICULATED?

The willingness to concentrate and "solve" the program into a single, box-like, volume, whether a private house, a gymnasium, a shed, a school, or a museum, has been a dominant tendency in Switzerland in the last decade. A similar trend has been observed elsewhere, particularly in Germany, Holland, and Belgium: the "Neue Einfachheit" (new simplicity) or the "Eenvoud" (unity, integrality). But we shall concentrate on the local Swiss scene, where such poetry has been explained by various and sometimes contradictory statements:

a) the request for the "ordinary" (a true borrowing from Venturi's word without the related images) connected to the refusal of the icon or the totem;

b) the ensuing rejection of architecture as a personal or idiosyncratic expression and the need for a "neutral" gesture;

c) the research of the essential in agreement with the social policy of "minimalism" rooted in the Swiss avant-garde tradition (Paul Artaria, Hans Schmidt, Emil Roth, Max Bill); and

d) the need for economy and "integrality" in response to sustainable development and energy-saving techniques.

Among these arguments, the more convincing ones were related to the philosophical tradition of materialism and the criticism of the industry of materials. The poetics and phenomenology of the physical and silent presence of the materials could even be related to a pun, a radical and political pun. This pun exists only in German. It was first uttered in the post-Dadaist and pre-Heideggerian Republic of Weimar: *Nicht darstellen sondern dastellen*. The act of representation (*darstellen*) is replaced by the immediate necessity to put things on the table now and here (*darstellen*).

Plain boxes were built and the photographers came to shoot laconic black-and-white pictures. The picturesque, one of the plagues of architecture in Switzerland, had been buried. The beautiful prosaic images of mere boxes became icons. The "magic box" of the camera would even infuse magic into "dematerialized" or "virtual" boxes.

If the "precept of the box" in Switzerland has been a reaction against "deconstruction" and "technological pathos," it is obvious that such a general assumption does not permit one to approach and study the singularity of each case. Nevertheless, one may agree that the challenge to build a single volume is directed to the revisiting of the modern tradition, Wright's "breaking of the box," Corbusier's comparative diagram of the "very difficult" compact solution, or the need for configuration (Gestaltung) expressed by Gropius and Hannes Meyer, of the ambivalent principle of "open is shut" contained in the Miesian pavilions. Indeed, the critical revisiting of the Modern movement has been the leading moral attitude in Swiss "learned" architecture over the last two decades. "Learned," that is self-conscious, architecture includes only about five percent of the overall building production in Switzerland, a percentage that corresponds to the situation observed elsewhere in Europe.

House in San Isidro, Argentina, 1988 (left); Espacité complex in La Chaux-de-Fonds, Switzerland, 1987–1995 (right).

THEIR BUILDINGS ARE ARTICULATED BOXES

The works of R&DR could be described as articulated boxes. The emphasis is given to the physical perception of the building. From the intimacy of the first sketches, a dominant line is followed in the hierarchy of the design: to create a sculptural event. The process of "composition" is a process in "configuration." This approach pays respect to the tradition of the Modern movement, but their ideological adhesion is based upon empiricism. Past adventures on the building site permit to integrate technical feasibility into the intimacy of the first sketches. It has been one of the leading precepts in the Swiss polytechnical training in architecture since Semper that building should rely upon previous practical experiences, that past mistakes and miscarriages on the building site should be digested and corrected, that risky gestures should be tamed.

The emphasis put on "the practical" (*das Praktische*) does not necessarily eliminate theory, even if the majority of the partisans of praticality strongly disbelieve in the necessity of intellectual speculation. Such a position submits theory to the apprenticeship and mastering of the technical and material processes. It means that theory enters the stage *a posteriori*, wearing the costume of the "professional" commentary on initial intentions. In this context, when time and history have been eliminated, the *a posteriori* is often delivered as the description of the initial intentions and plays the role of the *a priori*.

The belief in tekhné and "craft" can generate a lyrical narration of technology. It also permits to concentrate on "themes." "Themes in architecture" derive from the focussing on single, obsessive fragments. Their recurrence in design is stronger that formal evolution. Or rather, the possibility of formal evolution is connected to the industrial evolution and progress found in systems and technical devices put on the market by the industry of materials. The industry of materials also works with "specialities" and fragments.

THEIR THEMES IN ARCHITECTURE
What are the Richter and Dahl Rocha "themes in architecture"? Among their basic, obsessive preoccupations, certainly the mastering of natural light plays a leading role. They have observed Kahn's "construction of the light" in relationship to the dramatization of the structure. The lesson given by the master is linked with the shared memories of his last building at Yale. In their own designs, the "shafts" will integrate the courtyards, atriums, and staircases. Light is conducted as part of the circulation system. Effects of "literal transparency" cross the building both in vertical and horizontal directions. These modulations, which participate in the plastic organization of the light, are connected to the streams of passive solar energy. Richter and Dahl Rocha speak of "ecological approach" and tell us that "common sense prevails over technological sophistication," when the draft enters the drawing and the good old ventilation shaft questions the universal value of air-conditioning. Such empirical energy-saving devices have been tested on models at Lausanne by the Federal Institute of Technology. If light is a flux of energy, it stresses the physical, almost theatrical presence of the people moving within the building.

Train Maintenance Building,
Geneva, Switzerland, 1999
(this and opposite page).

From the inside we shall reach the outside of the box(es) and find a second "theme," best expressed by the Italian phrase promoted by Luciano Semerani and Boris Podrecca: *cultura del rivestimento*. That the cladding of a wall requires a revived "tectonical" culture has been one of the main assumptions put forward in the European architectural debate since the beginning of the nineties.

As a consequence to the successive "oil crises" that shook capitalism in the seventies, severe legal measures were adopted in Switzerland regarding the control of thermostatic waste, both in public and private buildings. According to the old capitalist logic, these new regulations were favorable to costly systems that produced a good crop of ugly and even pornographic façades, when

glass panels were proposed as the solution for isolating the internal structures and rooms. To the "learned" architects the new legal measures meant the necessity to revisit the construction of the peripheral walls. The modern routines of the "curtain" sustained by the framework of thin slabs and trusses or the single panel cast in concrete were questioned. Attention was directed to the system of the double wall. Various solutions were developed, from the self-supporting wall to the composed panel. Somehow, the technical metaphor of the skeleton was replaced by the sandwich. Whatever the solution, the problem of cladding was put forward.

Mario Botta is known for his clever epidermic use of brickwork or thin stone plates fixed on the masked wall that reflect to the public the image of brick or stone. For the architects who followed Ruskin's denunciation of "structural deceits" in his *Lamp of Truth* and reacted against the "false" image of a concrete wall clad with brick, the technical problem required further developments. A whole set of materials stood by at one's disposal: glass, ceramics, enameled steel sheets. The industry of materials had anticipated the situation. Some architects developed their own preferences and used corrugated iron, wood tiles, wood siding, eternit sheets, concrete panels on reinforced concrete walls. Two basic problems were put forward: the control of the joint and the personal, moral adhesion to one material in rejecting others. As in the case of the brick or corrugated iron, strong and "ancient" connotations were attached to the materials now used in cladding. The network of the joint could alter if not dilapidate the visual mass inscribed in the volume. Would the face be a screen, a gate, a mask? Would the underwear become the suit?

In contrast to other colleagues, Richter and Dahl Rocha do not show a constant personal preference for the materials exposed in cladding. They rather use a set of contrasted solutions; they want to blend, for instance, steel plates and stone panels in the case of the EOS headquarters in Lausanne. The choice is adapted to the "character" and scale of the building. The perception of the image is simultaneous with the perception of the mass. The skin takes roots in the configuration of the box(es). A genuine understanding of the various technical systems makes it possible to translate the sensory into the sensual.

ELEGANCE AND HEDONISM

The physical, concrete presence of the material leads to the question: Can elegance be a theme in architecture? Is elegance a futile category, tied to fashion and quick obsolescence? Is it moral? Is it not a slogan developed by the motor-car industry? Does it reduce architecture to a mere rhetoric of seduction? What has it got to do with the cultural value of architecture? Is elegance addressed to the client? Does it add brilliance to the public institution? Does it enhance the corporate identity of the client? Is it linked to the aesthetics of pleasure?

Richter and Dahl Rocha admit: "We use elegance." And they tell you boldly that elegance is not tied to fashion and obsolescence, but to permanency and the negation of temporariness. This statement can be related to their own pleasure in designing profiles, joints, cornices and canopies. The metaphor of architecture as sculpture must be recalled because they work in Lausanne, where Jean Tschumi was active both as a professor and a practicing architect. A direct link could be traced between Jean Tschumi and Richter and Dahl Rocha, not only because Richter's father worked with Tschumi but also because Richter and Dahl Rocha have looked at Tschumi's work "from the outside," without being influenced by the many local prejudices and anecdotes. The lesson found in Tschumi was useful in two directions, first in urban design (the scale, the articulation, and the position of the building are the tools for city planning), second in technology (the necessity to learn, master, and confront the numerous catalogues published by the building industry). For Tschumi, formal elegance resulted from technical sophistication and the mastering of the details.

Richter and Dahl Rocha's hedonism in buildings is linked to a subtle use of the pleasure delivered by the materials. It does not lift moderation to the level of a philosophical principle in life. The tactile impression offers a sensual play of contrasts and surprises.

EOS Headquarters in Lausanne, Switzerland, 1995 (opposite page); Nestlé Headquarters, Jean Tschumi Architect, Vevey, Switzerland, 1960 (top); Nestlé Headquarters Renovation, 1996–2000 (bottom).

Brick-Brick ▶

House in Tortuguitas

Completed in 1986 as the architect's residence, the house is situated on a flat, wooded, low-density residential area in the province of Buenos Aires. It appears from the outside as a solid, naked, monolithic brick block, even though large windows and a big terrace provide a generous interior-exterior relationship at the ground level. The purity of this volume is only contaminated and therefore reinforced by a few details like the setback of the windows revealing the thickness of the wall at the ground level, the cornice, or the "decorative" use of the drainpipes in the corners. The rigid composition of the plans contrasts with the highly articulated sections that allow for different heights according to the proportion and hierarchy of the rooms. Built with a low budget, its design intentionally follows the logic of a simple technology: bearing brick walls stuccoed on the inside, steel windows and a standard light prefabricated system of concrete beams and ceramic blocks for the intermediate slab and the roof. The exterior works including the terrace floor, the low walls, and the steps were all done with the same bricks.

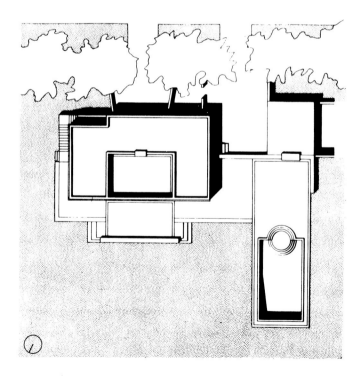

1. ENTRY
2. HALL
3. LIBRARY/PANTRY
4. KITCHEN
5. DINING ROOM
6. LIVING ROOM
7. STUDY
8. GUEST ROOM
9. HALL
10. BEDROOM
11. MASTER BEDROOM

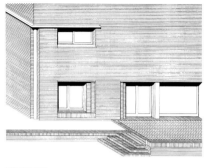

AXONOMETRIC

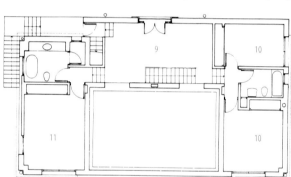

SECOND FLOOR PLAN

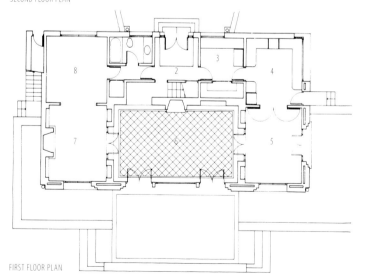

FIRST FLOOR PLAN

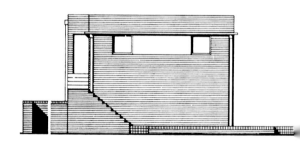

WEST ELEVATION

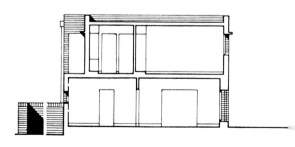

SECTION LOOKING EAST

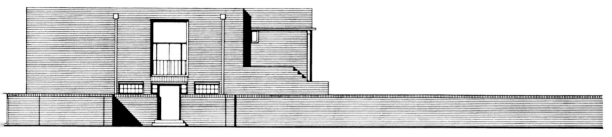

SOUTH ELEVATION

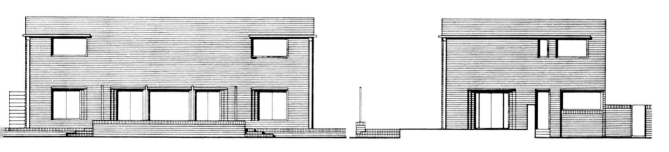

NORTH ELEVATION

EAST ELEVATION

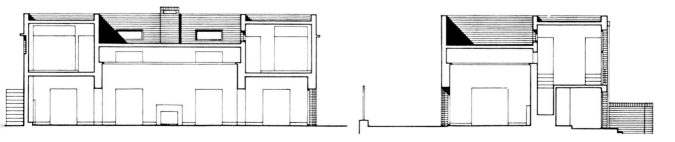

SECTION LOOKING SOUTH

SECTION LOOKING WEST

House in San Isidro

Situated in the residential area of San Isidro, some 12.5 miles (20 kilometers) away from the center of Buenos Aires, this three-story house was built on a wooded plot sloping down slightly toward the Rio de la Plata. The living room, the dining room, and the kitchen are on the top floor, which offers the best views. The main floor is made up of the hall, the stairs leading to the upper floor, and the bedrooms with their bathrooms. On the lower floor are the service rooms and the garage. In response to the topography of the site, the house is built against a big retaining wall, therefore only opening onto three sides, and adapts to the slope by means of a series of terraces, stairs, and walls that emphasize the horizontal stratification of the composition. The thick exterior brick walls host the independent, non-revealed concrete structure, the roller blinds, and the big sliding aluminum windows on the upper floor.

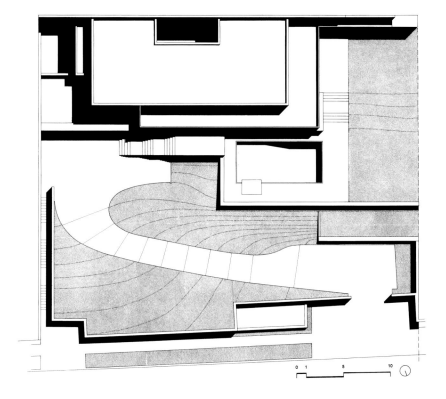

0 1   5   10

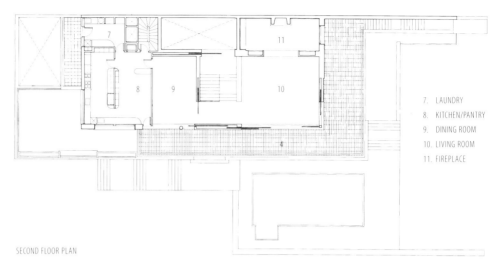

SECOND FLOOR PLAN

7. LAUNDRY
8. KITCHEN/PANTRY
9. DINING ROOM
10. LIVING ROOM
11. FIREPLACE

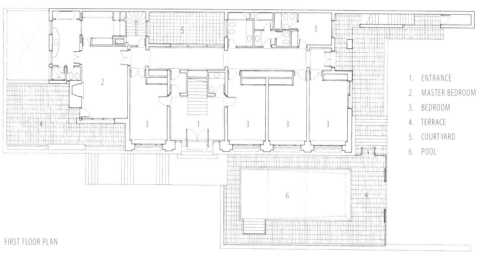

FIRST FLOOR PLAN

1. ENTRANCE
2. MASTER BEDROOM
3. BEDROOM
4. TERRACE
5. COURTYARD
6. POOL

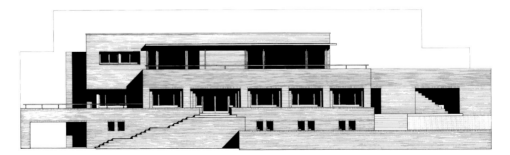

NORTH ELEVATION

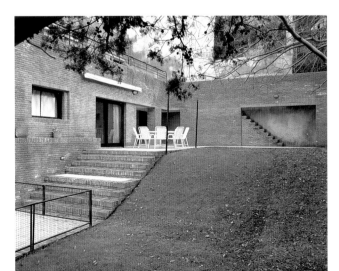

The master bedroom's terrace (top) and the west terrace on the first floor (middle and bottom) with stairs leading down to the pool and up to the main floor. The north elevation, facing the sun and the river views (overleaf), shows the volume that opens generously on the top floor with the living areas, reduces openings on the middle level of the bedrooms, and finally dissolves into the slope through the oversized entrance stairs.

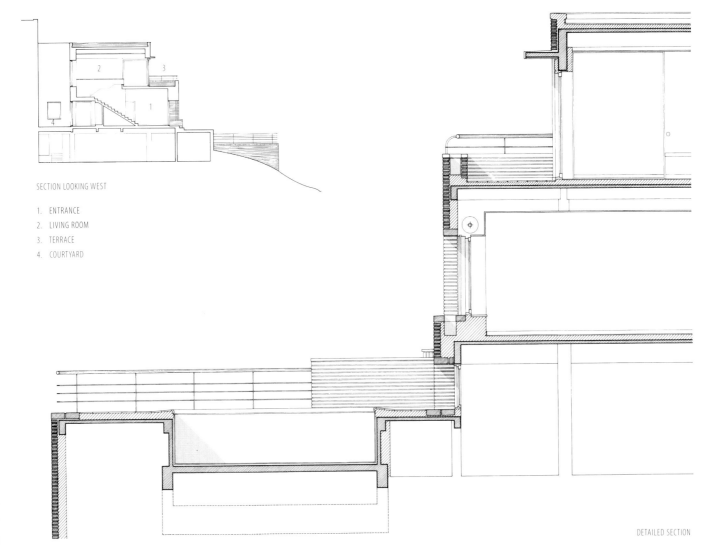

SECTION LOOKING WEST

1. ENTRANCE
2. LIVING ROOM
3. TERRACE
4. COURTYARD

DETAILED SECTION

Stucco-Metal ▶

House in Lutry

This house is located in the region east of Lausanne, set in the middle of sloping vineyards. It faces a magnificent view of Lake Geneva and a complete panorama of the Alps. To allow for the best views, the living areas were situated on the top floor, while the bedrooms and bathrooms occupy the middle level, leaving the service areas below. A linear staircase starting below and ending at the top level becomes a major element in the composition. The wing-shaped roof, suspended above the living room, stands out against the landscape and balances the natural light arriving from either side. The outside walls of the house's main body were intended to closely resemble the surrounding vineyard terraces.

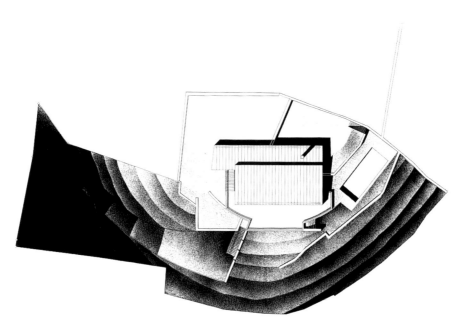

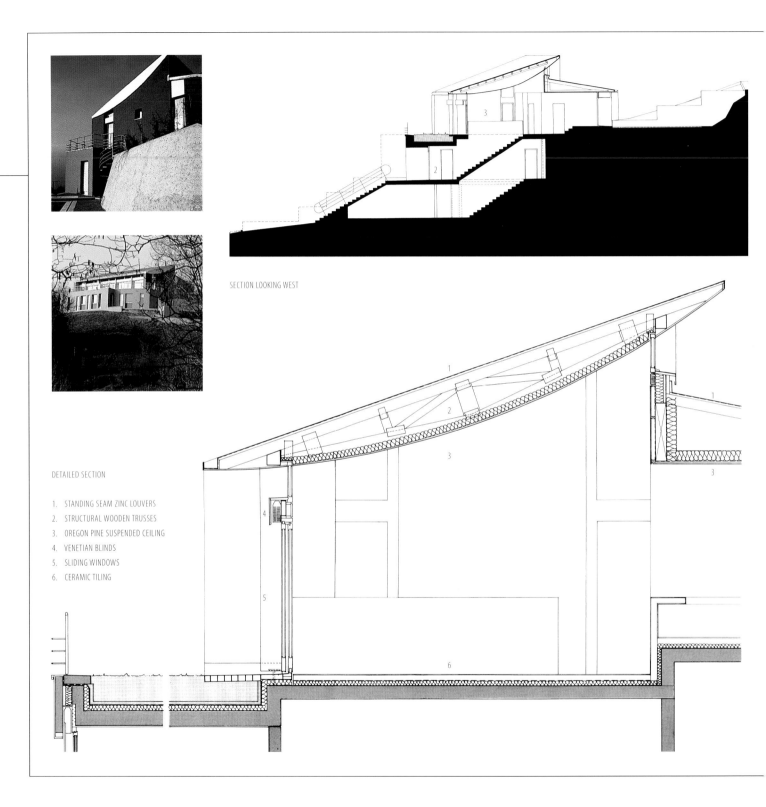

SECTION LOOKING WEST

DETAILED SECTION

1. STANDING SEAM ZINC LOUVERS
2. STRUCTURAL WOODEN TRUSSES
3. OREGON PINE SUSPENDED CEILING
4. VENETIAN BLINDS
5. SLIDING WINDOWS
6. CERAMIC TILING

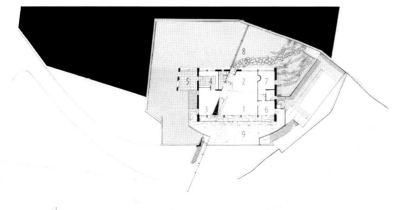

1. LIVING ROOM
2. FIREPLACE
3. DINING ROOM
4. KITCHEN
5. COVERED TERRACE
6. STUDY
7. GUEST ROOM
8. NORTH COURT
9. GRASS TERRACE

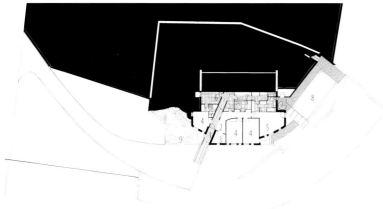

LOWER PLAN

1. ENTRANCE
2. HALL
3. CLOAKROOM
4. BEDROOMS
5. PARENTS' BEDROOM
6. LAUNDRY
7. STORAGE SPACE
8. SWIMMING POOL
9. BIOTOPE TERRACE

BASEMENT PLAN

1. GARAGE
2. SERVICE ENTRANCE
3. TECHNICAL ROOM
4. CELLARS, FALLOUT SHELTER, DEPOTS

Espacité

Developed after a competition of ideas was launched in 1987 for the celebration of the one hundredth anniversary of Le Corbusier's birth in La Chaux-de-Fonds, the complex of Espacité proposes to redevelop the "Place sans Nom" (the Nameless Square), an empty urban space that emerged after a series of demolitions. Three elements participate to restructure and enliven the site: a square that opens onto the Avenue Léopold Robert; a bar building housing shops, offices, and flats; and an office tower with the Tourist Bureau on the ground floor, a coffee bar and a public observation gallery on the top floor, and offices on the remaining levels. The dialogue between the two main elements of the composition, the tower and the bar building, contributes to the definition of the public square renamed "Place Le Corbusier." At the town's scale the bar building restores the urban fabric while acknowledging its very characteristic longitudinal structure, and the tower—urban sign and observation point above the town—balances the masses of the high buildings already existing on the Avenue Léopold Robert.

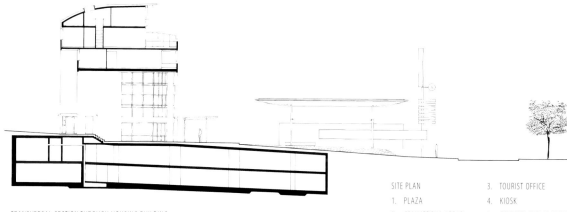

TRANSVERSAL SECTION THROUGH HOUSING BUILDING

SITE PLAN   3. TOURIST OFFICE

1. PLAZA   4. KIOSK

2. COMMERCIAL AREAS   5. COVERED PUBLIC FORUM

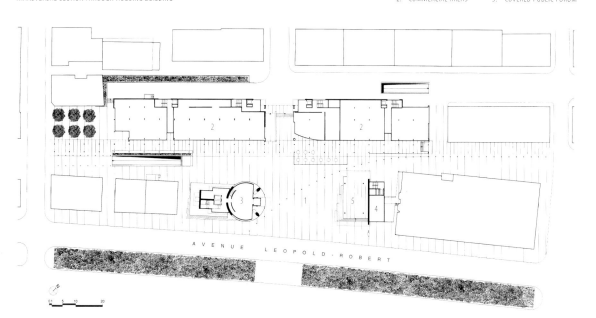

AVENUE LEOPOLD-ROBERT

0.1 5 10 20

AXONOMETRIC VIEW

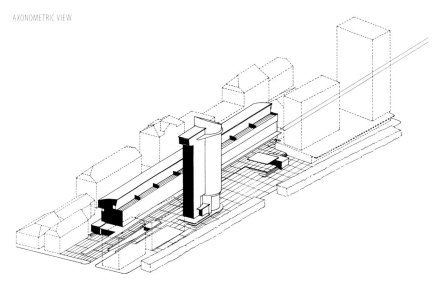

Views of the "Le Corbusier" plaza, animated by the tourist office at the base of the tower, the forum (foreground, top), and the shops on the ground level of the bar building (bottom). The urban scale opening in this bar building links the plaza with the surrounding residential area.

The tower, a "tall house" in the European tradition with its cylindrical office area and service shaft, articulated to enhance the overall impression of slenderness. The axonometric drawing shows the mixed structure, the floors on a perimetral steel construction on the concrete table base and suspended mezzanine.

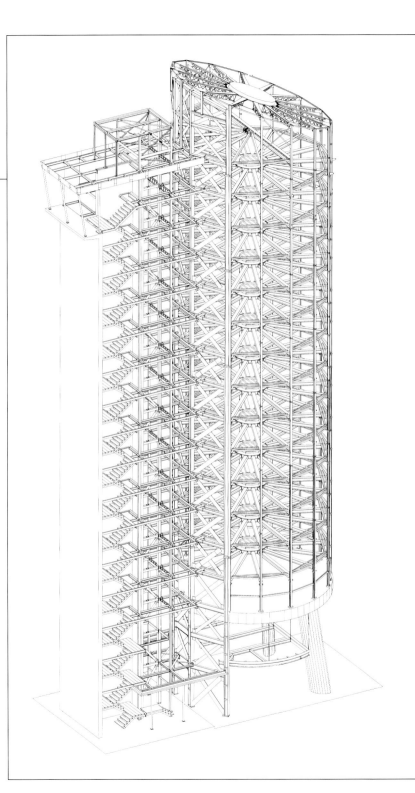

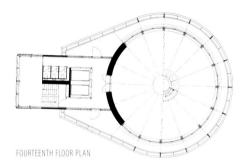

FOURTEENTH FLOOR PLAN

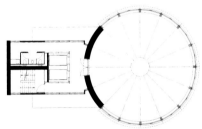

TYPICAL FLOOR PLAN

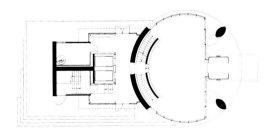

GROUND FLOOR PLAN

The radial steel slabs installed during construction (this page) allowed for an additional staircase to be added if needed. Also shown are views of the restaurant's terrace and belvedere on the back (opposite).

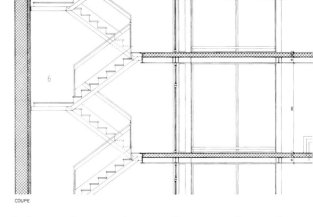

COUPE

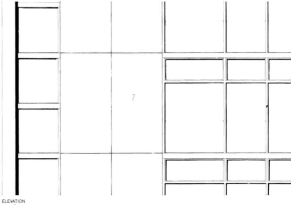

ELEVATION

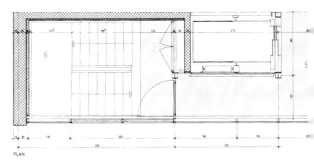

PLAN

1. EXTRUDED ALUMINUM PANELS
   VENTILATED AIR SPACE
   THERMAL INSULATION
   PREFABRICATED CONCRETE ELEMENTS
2. FOLDED STEEL SHEET
   BAKED RESIN FINISH
3. DOUBLE-GLAZED ALUMINUM WINDOWS

   EXTERIOR ROLL BLIND
4. TILE CARPET ON ACCESS FLOOR
5. PVC FLOOR FINISH ON SCREEN
6. SERVICE STAIRS—ALUMINUM SHEET
   STEPS ON STEEL CONSTRUCTION
   ENAMEL PAINT FINISH
7. ALUCOBOND PANELS BAKED RESIN FINISH

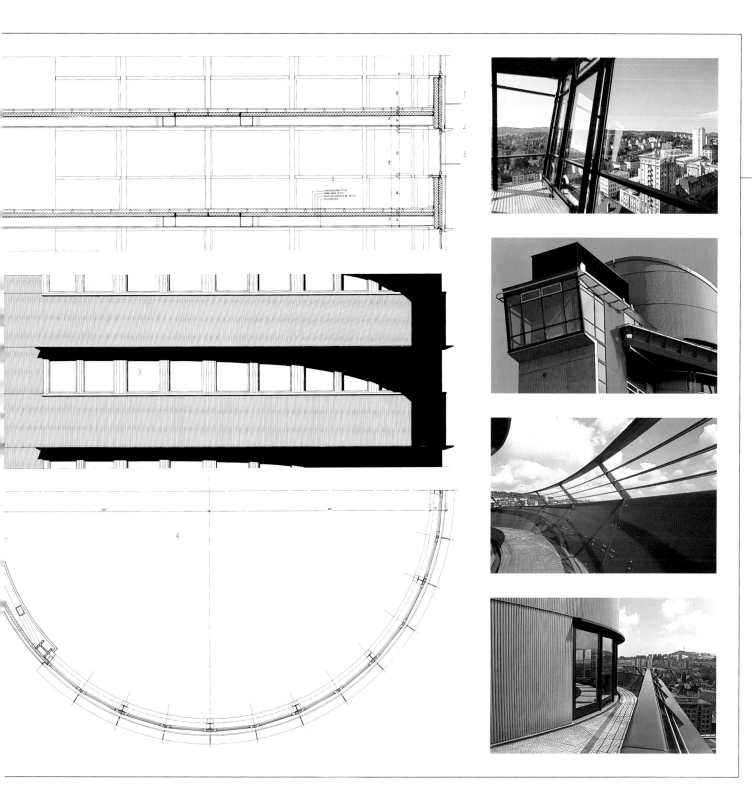

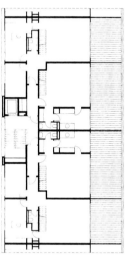

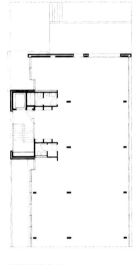

FOURTH FLOOR PLAN

THIRD FLOOR PLAN

FIRST FLOOR PLAN

A view from the southwest showing the long bar building with shops and covered walkway on the ground floor and the setback of the apartments (top). The plans show the different apartment configurations and office spaces (middle). Also shown are views of the staircase in the rear (bottom and opposite).

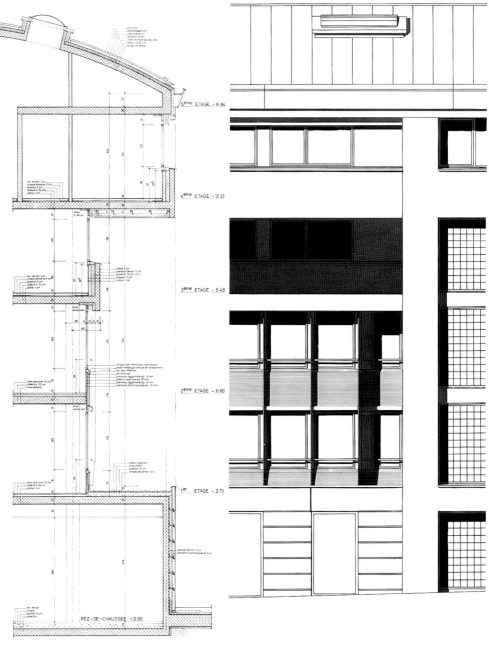

HOUSING BUILDING—DETAILED SECTION THROUGH NORTHWEST FAÇADE

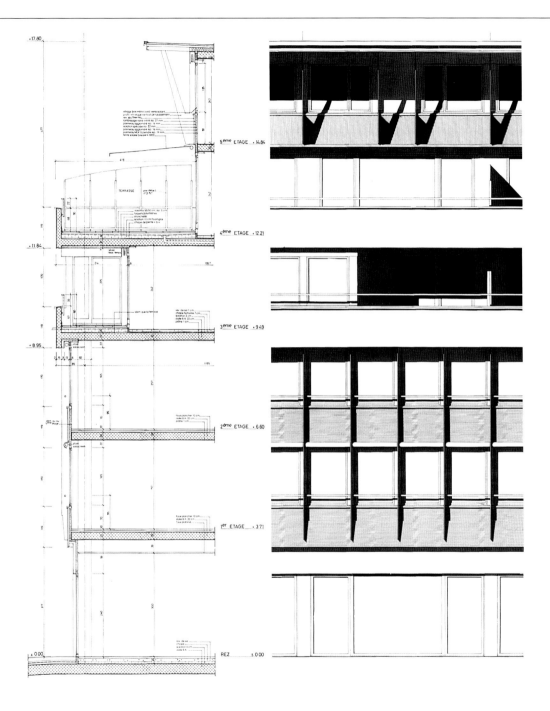

HOUSING BUILDING—DETAILED SECTION THROUGH SOUTHEAST FAÇADE

Details of the front (this page) and rear façades (opposite) show the horizontal layering of the bar building, each of which expresses a different functions: entrances and glazed shop windows on the ground level, curtain walls for the offices and stuccoed façades for the apartments.

FAE Contemporary Art Museum

The Museum of Contemporary Art was set up on the shores of Lake Geneva, in Pully, in the eastern outskirts of Lausanne. Two ancient buildings, which date back to the beginning of the century and which sheltered the "Teintureries Lyonnaises," were standing on the site. Their architectural and spatial qualities justified their preservation and transformation. The main neoclassical building has retained its administrative calling and accommodates offices, the bookshop, and the storage for works of art. The second building with industrial features enables the installation of a string of exhibition rooms of varying sizes. The sole modern intervention was the low body, which articulates the two buildings and houses the main entrance and reception to the museum. Its roof has been treated as a sculptural terrace and constitutes the final stage of the visit through the exhibition rooms. Its architectural treatment asserts the contemporary intervention, serves as a mark for the visitor, and strengthens the new museum's general identity.

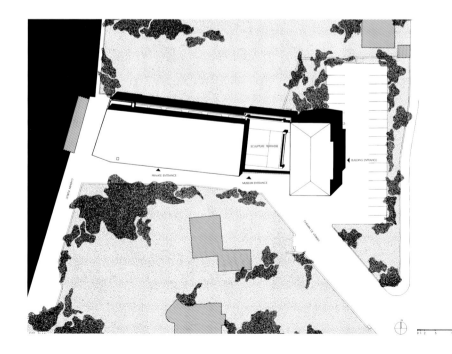

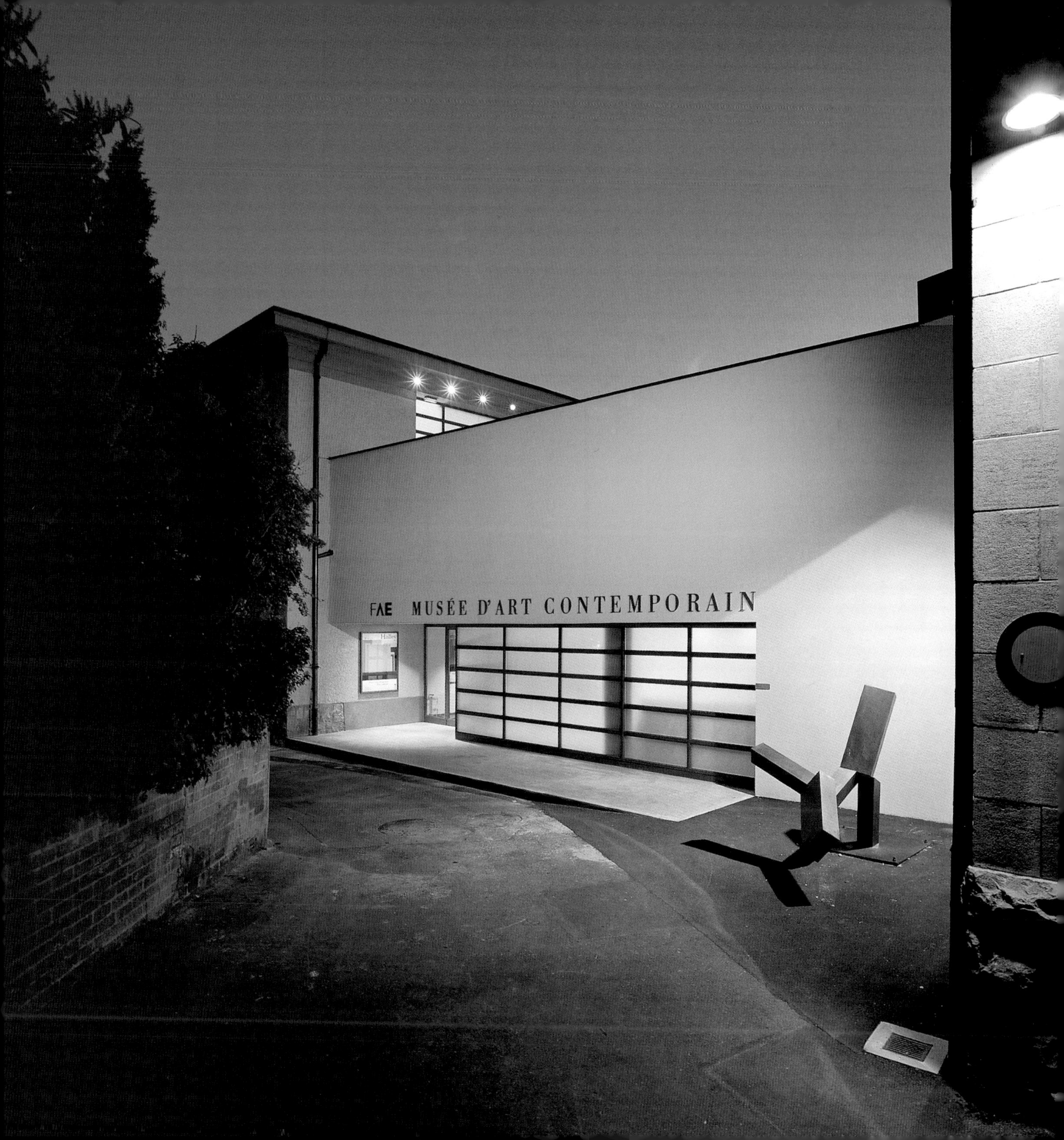
FAE MUSÉE D'ART CONTEMPORAIN

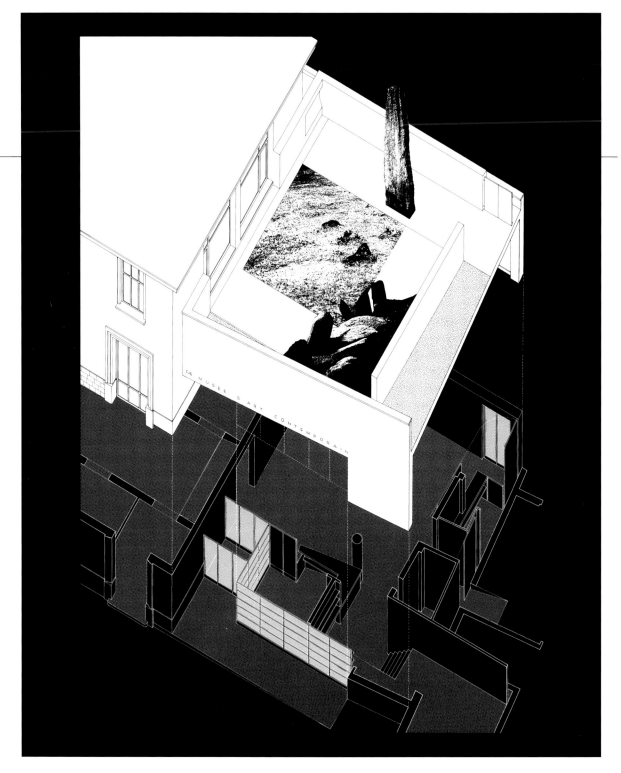

An axonometric view shows the
added construction that articulates
the two existing buildings, with the
entrance area on the ground floor and
an enclosed sculpture terrace above.

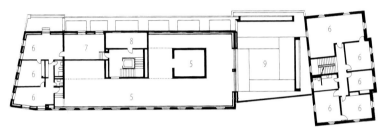

SECOND FLOOR PLAN

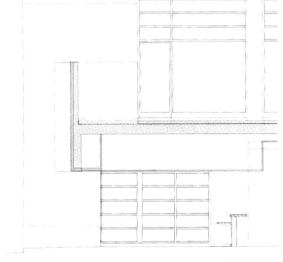

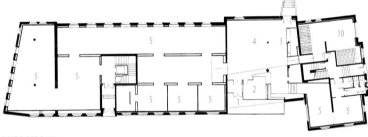

FIRST FLOOR PLAN

DETAILED SECTION

1. ENTRANCE
2. TICKET OFFICE
3. CAFE
4. HALL
5. EXHIBITION SPACE
6. OFFICES
7. MEETING ROOM
8. TECHNICAL
9. SCULPTURE TERRACE
10. ART STORAGE

EAST ELEVATION

Housing Building in Prilly

Located in Prilly, in the outskirts to the west of Lausanne, this building comprises fifty-seven apartments, essentially of two, three, and four rooms. Two underground levels house parking spaces for sixty-four vehicles and a complex for civil protection (shelters, waiting station, and sanitary post). To the urban code's restrictions the building responds by embracing the form of the landscape, adapting to the slope and articulating a series of private terraces. The ground floor's transparency allows it to link the higher and lower sides of the site, playing on the contrast between the convex and more closed façade behind and the concave façade open to the sun and view.

01   5   10

FIFTH LEVEL PLAN

GROUND FLOOR

Housing Building in Prilly

TRANSVERSAL SECTION

Sketch and details of west façade
(this page), and an overall view of
same façade opening generously
towards the views and the lake
(following page). At the foot of the
building lies a sculpture by Swiss
artist Olivier Estoppey (previous page).

Detail of the eastern façade showing
the main entrance and the more
contained openings for the bedrooms.

1. RENDERED REINFORCED CONCRETE
2. VENETIAN BLIND AND PAINTED STEEL COVER
3. DOUBLE-GLAZED WOOD/ALUMINUM WINDOW FRAME
4. GLASS BRICKS

General view of the eastern façade
that bends away from the slope and
allows for the entrance area (opposite).
Also shown are details of the internal
staircases, acknowledged in the apartments (top) or through the glass-block
wall on the ground floor (bottom).

Brick-Wood ▶

Swhome Housing Concept

Developed from the prized project of the first Europan session in 1988, the Swhome concept aims at promoting the building of economic, modular, evolutive, and easily convertible flats (do-it-yourself). The original idea—developed for individual housing—led to a system for collective habitat, the Swhome-Building, which has been the basis for several projects in Switzerland. Among recurrent themes of architectural debate in recent years, the Swhome system aims at exploring and following up certain leads, including how to reconcile the intention to create an open plan, allowing for the inhabitant's aspirations to personalization, with the standardized and industrialized requirements of construction. The development of concrete solutions meant going beyond the ordinary architectural and technical framework by redefining the roles played by the different actors in the housing production process (inhabitants, architects, engineers, builders, and developers).

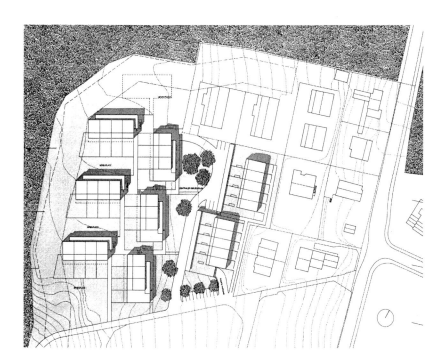

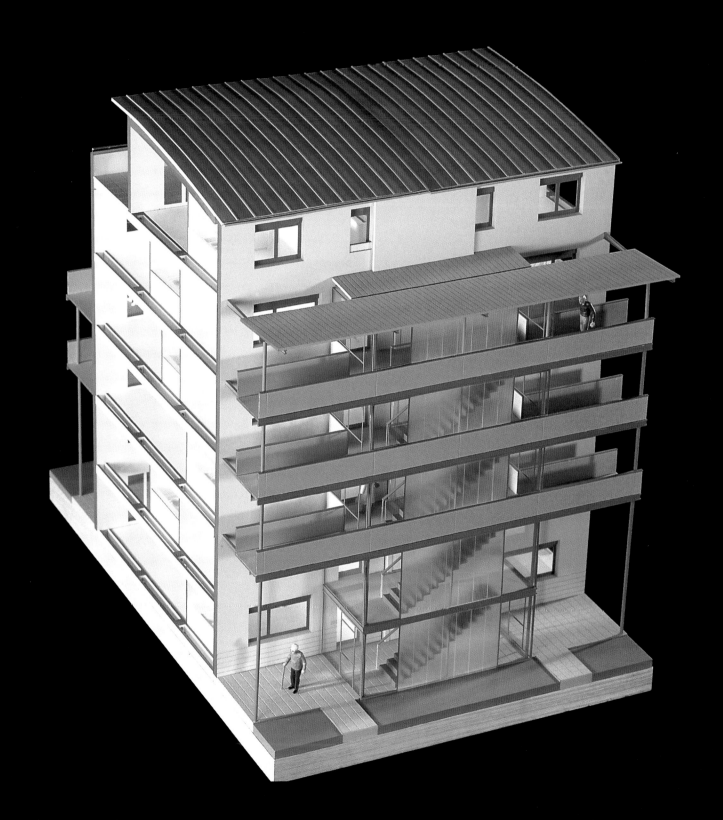

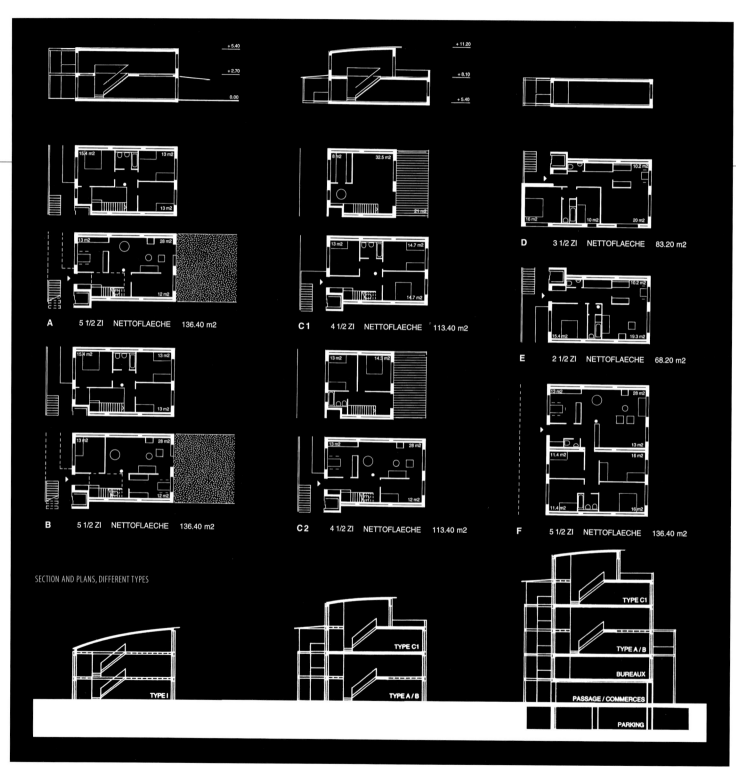

+ 5.40
+ 2.70
0.00

+ 11.20
+ 8.10
+ 5.40

15.4 m2   13 m2
            13 m2

13 m2   28 m2
            12 m2

A   5 1/2 ZI   NETTOFLAECHE   136.40 m2

8 m2   32.5 m2
            21 m2

13 m2   14.7 m2
            14.7 m2

C 1   4 1/2 ZI   NETTOFLAECHE   113.40 m2

10.2 m2
16 m2   10 m2   20 m2

D   3 1/2 ZI   NETTOFLAECHE   83.20 m2

10.2 m2
15.4 m2   19.3 m2

E   2 1/2 ZI   NETTOFLAECHE   68.20 m2

15.4 m2   13 m2
            13 m2

13 m2   28 m2
            12 m2

B   5 1/2 ZI   NETTOFLAECHE   136.40 m2

13 m2   14.3 m2

13 m2   28 m2
            12 m2

C 2   4 1/2 ZI   NETTOFLAECHE   113.40 m2

13 m2   28 m2
            13 m2
11.4 m2   16 m2
11.4 m2   16 m2

F   5 1/2 ZI   NETTOFLAECHE   136.40 m2

SECTION AND PLANS, DIFFERENT TYPES

TYPE I

TYPE C1

TYPE A / B

TYPE C1

TYPE A / B

BUREAUX

PASSAGE / COMMERCES

PARKING

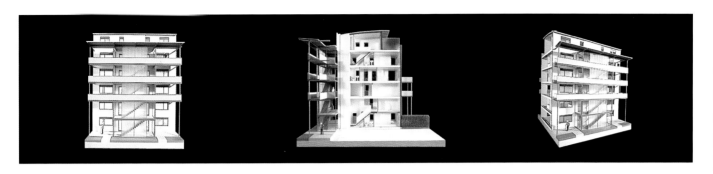

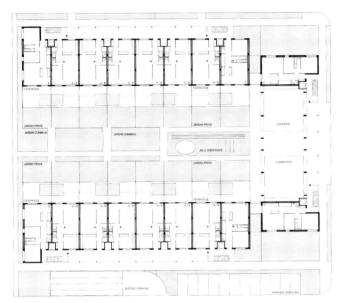

GROUND FLOOR PLAN, URBAN TYPE

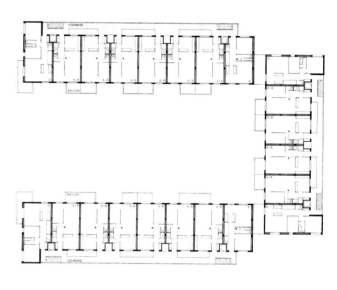

TYPICAL FLOOR PLAN, URBAN TYPE

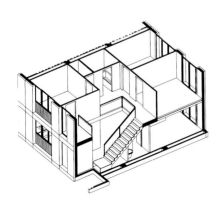

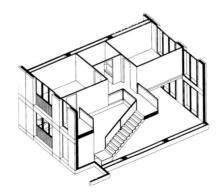

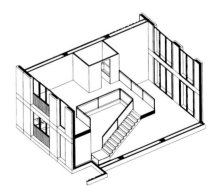

AXONOMETRIC DRAWINGS, TYPE A/B

Houses in Chailly

These two semidetached houses in Chailly, a residential area of Lausanne, can be considered the first built example of the Swhome "Villa" housing concept, even though this system was conceived for a row-house typology. According to the principles of the system and starting from a fixed basic design, the clients were able to choose their own interior arrangement and finishings. Two different materials were used on the exterior in order to break down the impact of the three-story level: ceramic brick for the lower levels and red cedar wood panels on the top floor, protected by the roof eaves. Unlike the case of the row-house typology in which the units open towards the front and rear elevation only, in the case of this semidetached scheme, current in Switzerland, they open sideways as well. This fact is recognized by the special care in the lateral elevation design and by placing the main exterior space in front of it. This space is also defined by a single-story annex that houses the functions currently found in a basement.

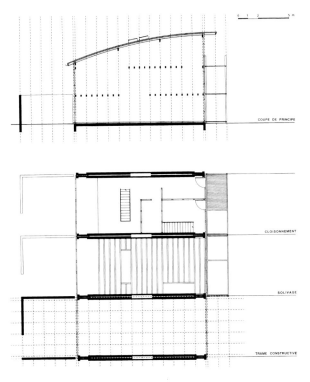

COUPE DE PRINCIPE

CLOISONNEMENT

SOLIVAGE

TRAME CONSTRUCTIVE

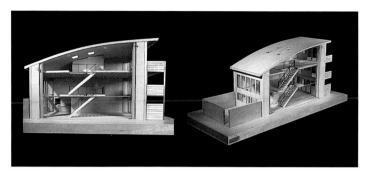

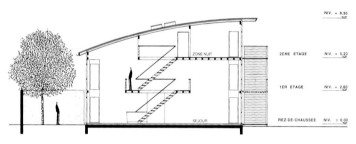

NIV. + 8.30

ZONE NUIT

2EME ETAGE   NIV. + 5.20

1ER ETAGE   NIV. + 2.60

SEJOUR

REZ-DE-CHAUSSEE   NIV. ± 0.00

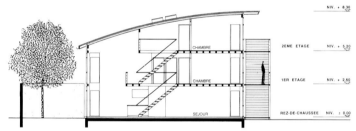

NIV. + 8.30

CHAMBRE

2EME ETAGE   NIV. + 5.20

CHAMBRE

1ER ETAGE   NIV. + 2.60

SEJOUR

REZ-DE-CHAUSSEE   NIV. ± 0.00

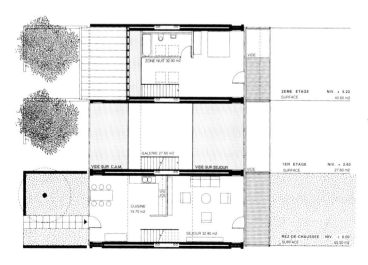

VIDE

ZONE NUIT 32.00 m2

2EME ETAGE   NIV. + 5.20
SURFACE   40.60 m2

GALERIE 27.60 m2

VIDE SUR C.A.M.   VIDE SUR SEJOUR   VIDE

1ER ETAGE   NIV. + 2.60
SURFACE   27.60 m2

CUISINE
19.70 m2

SEJOUR 32.80 m2

REZ-DE-CHAUSSEE   NIV. ± 0.00
SURFACE   65.50 m2

SECTION AND PLANS, VILLA TYPE (ONE ROOM)

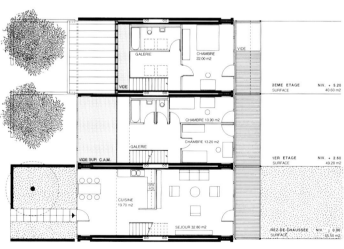

GALERIE   CHAMBRE
22.00 m2

VIDE

2EME ETAGE   NIV. + 5.20
SURFACE   40.60 m2

CHAMBRE 10.90 m2

CHAMBRE 13.20 m2

GALERIE

VIDE SUR C.A.M.

1ER ETAGE   NIV. + 2.60
SURFACE   49.20 m2

CUISINE
19.70 m2

SEJOUR 32.80 m2

REZ-DE-CHAUSSEE   NIV. ± 0.00
SURFACE   65.50 m2

SECTION AND PLANS, VILLA TYPE (TWO ROOMS)

0 1 2   5 m

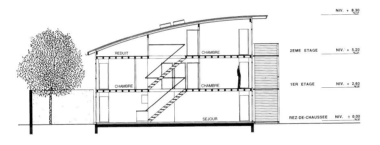

		NIV. + 8.30
REDUIT	CHAMBRE	
		2EME ETAGE NIV. + 5.20
CHAMBRE	CHAMBRE	
		1ER ETAGE NIV. + 2.60
	SEJOUR	REZ-DE-CHAUSSEE NIV. ± 0.00

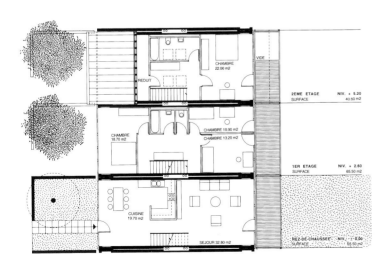

CHAMBRE 22.00 m2 · REDUIT · VIDE

2EME ETAGE   NIV. + 5.20
SURFACE   40.60 m2

CHAMBRE 18.70 m2 · CHAMBRE 10.90 m2 · CHAMBRE 13.20 m2

1ER ETAGE   NIV. + 2.60
SURFACE   65.50 m2

CUISINE 19.70 m2 · SEJOUR 32.80 m2

REZ-DE-CHAUSSEE   NIV. ± 0.00
SURFACE   65.50 m2

SECTION AND PLANS, VILLA TYPE (THREE ROOMS)

The model shows the basic fixed design of the three-story volume (opposite, top). The different layouts show the flexibility of possible configurations in plan and section.

Simplicity, generosity, and intimacy of interior spaces is created with whitened concrete block wall, smooth plastered ceilings, and beechwood floors and staircase.

Forest Refuge

VALLEE DE JOUX, VAUD, SWITZERLAND

The forest refuge offers a shelter for the hikers in the Grand Risoux forest in the Jura mountains. With rustic comfort, it is furnished with only a table and wood stove. The initial brief proposed the development of a constructive principle allowing the forestry agents to pre-construct the different elements during the winter, while waiting for the return of spring for their assembly. The whole was built in fir—a material traditionally used in the region—including the roof's shingles. Starting from the traditional cabin type and keeping its basic elements, the project operates a series of geometrical transformations: the corners are unblocked and the wall slides out following the strategy of the modern plan; the rotation created is followed by a shift of the roof system; and the eaves articulate the two geometries. The result is a rather organic volume in tune with the landscape.

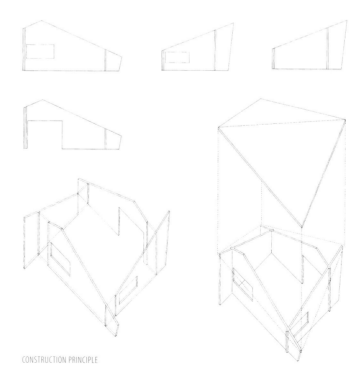

CONSTRUCTION PRINCIPLE

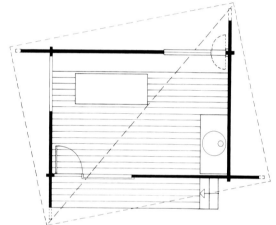

PLAN

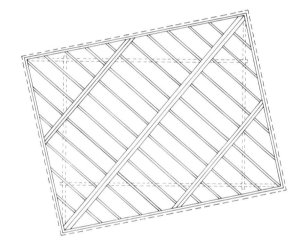

ROOF STRUCTURE

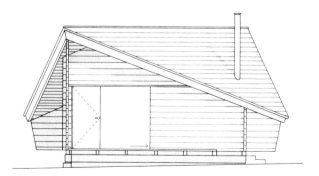

EAST ELEVATION

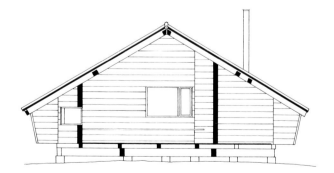

SECTION

School of Agriculture in Grange-Verney

Organized by the state of Vaud in 1989, the competition encompassed the extension of the college and the cantonal agricultural station of Grange-Verney, to be made into a new vocational training center for agricultural work. The program is composed of classrooms, workshops for teaching and maintenance, and a multi-purpose gymnasium as well as a fallout shelter. This project, which won third prize, strengthens both the identity and the image of the new center, in particular through its implantation that allows for the redefinition of the composition's overall scale and to control the outdoor spaces. The treatment of volume and materials (concrete, stone, wood) contributes to this end and establishes a dialogue between the existing and the future parts.

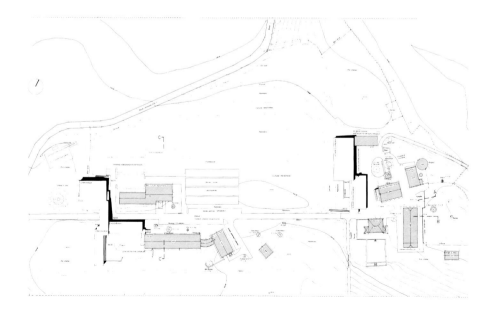

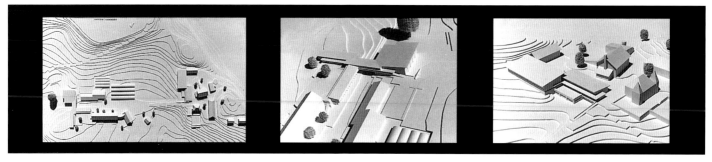

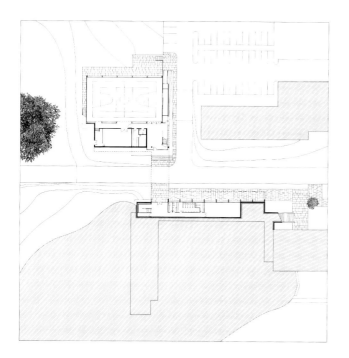

LOWER GROUND FLOOR

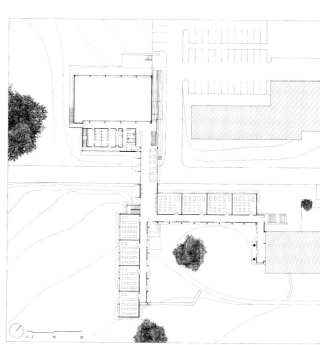

UPPER GROUND FLOOR

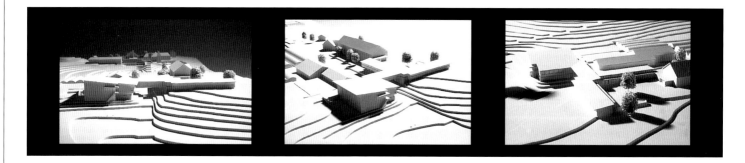

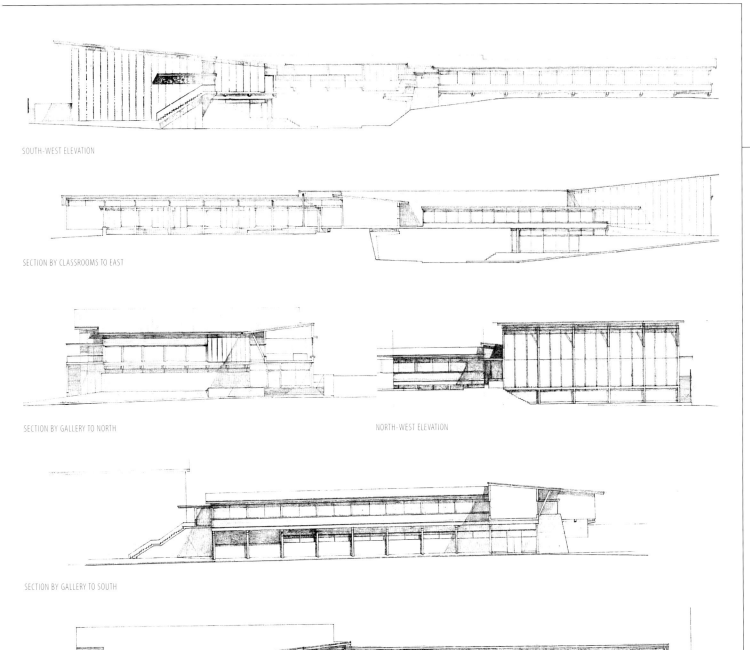

SOUTH-WEST ELEVATION

SECTION BY CLASSROOMS TO EAST

SECTION BY GALLERY TO NORTH

NORTH-WEST ELEVATION

SECTION BY GALLERY TO SOUTH

SECTION BY CLASSROOMS TO NORTH

Wood-Metal ▶

Jumbo Shopping Mall

This project consists of the total remodeling of a commercial center originally built in 1973, and the addition of 54,000 square feet (5,000 square meters) of commercial space and increased parking capacity. This intervention allowed for the redefinition of the building's identity. Thus the new red cedar façade covers both the existing body and the new extension, unifying the whole. The dynamism of this thousand-foot (three-hundred-meter) façade, curving along the street, is emphasized by its horizontal composition. In contrast with this light wooden envelope, and articulated by the entrance level's glazed façade, the downward slope of the road reveals a heavy brick-clad basement.

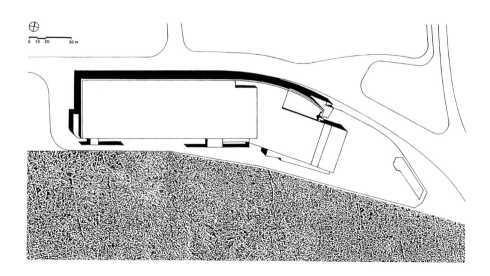

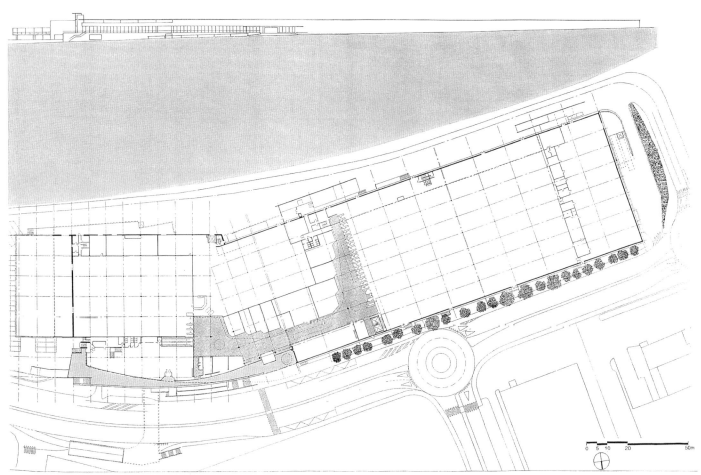

ELEVATION AND GROUND FLOOR PLAN

0 5 10 20 50m

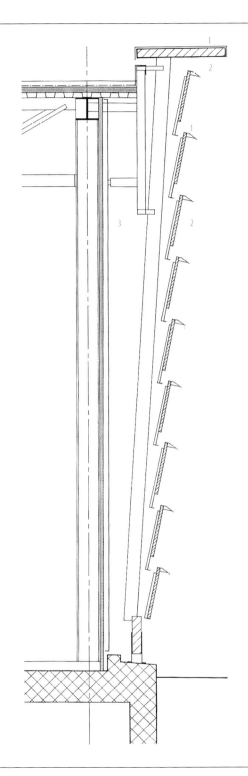

1. ALUMINUM SHEETING WITH BAKED RESIN FINISH
2. RED CEDAR BOARDING
3. CORRUGATED STEEL SHEETING WITH BAKED RESIN FINISH

Detailed section of the new red cedar boarding that covers the existing corrugated steel cladding. The wooden boarding is protected by a wide metal cornice at the very top and smaller ones in between, enhancing the horizontality of the new covering.

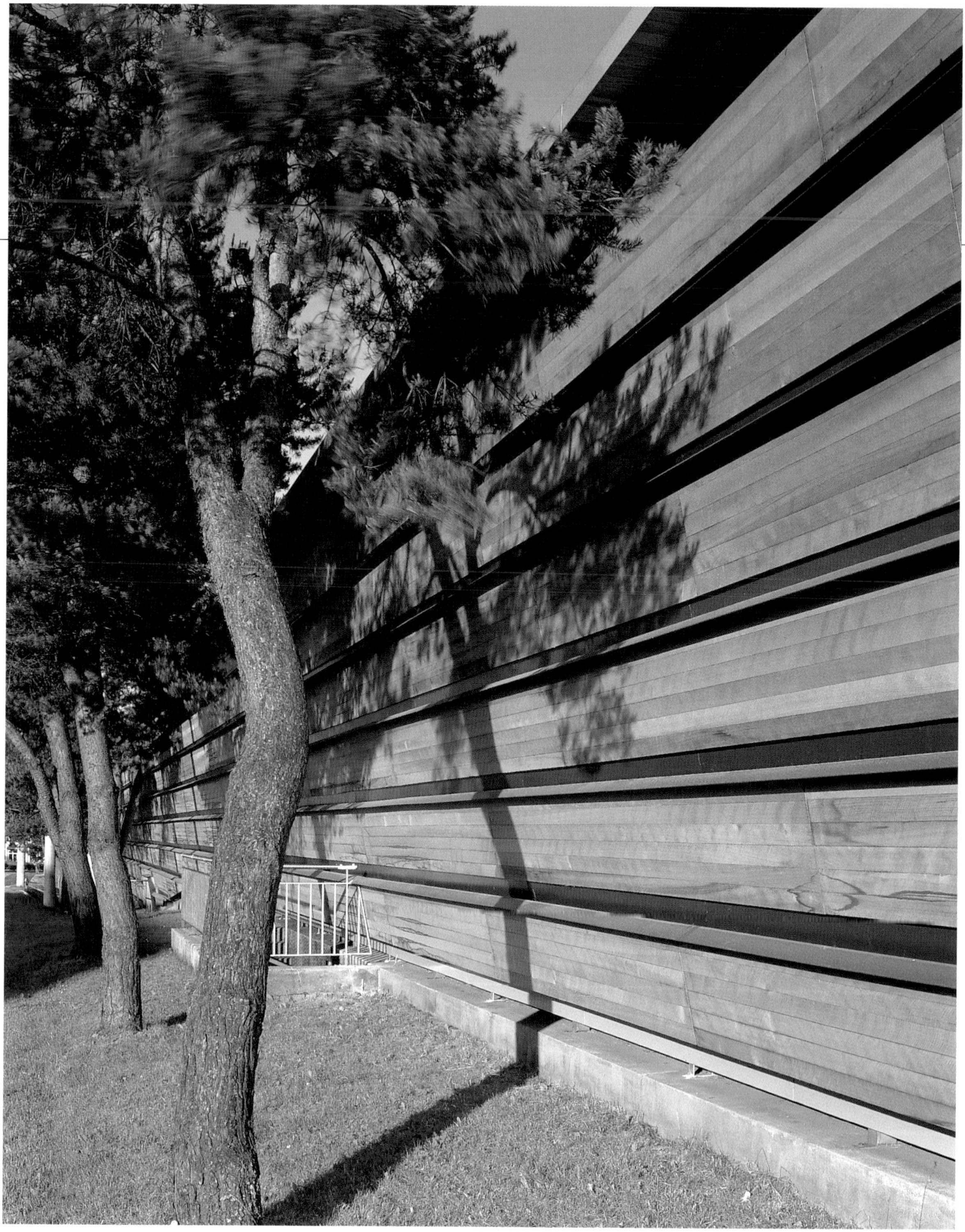

View of the existing building with its new covering (opposite) and the extension with new entrance (this page), all of which is unified by the new wooden wrapping.

Train Maintenance Building

Located in the immediate surroundings of Geneva's train station, the center consists of a building exceeding 108,000 square feet (10,000 square meters) for the maintenance of the latest reclinable train configurations, as well as a service annex. The plain architectural idiom rests on the materials own expression and reinforces the functional character of the building. The main façades (one thousand feet/three hundred meters long) are clad in oversized wood shingles and are protected by very wide eaves, which in turn contrast with the aluminum end façades, creating a certain tension when they meet at an angle. In fact, their intersection suggests a section rather than a corner, as if the different naves, sliding against each other, had no precise end; as if they could move along the tracks.

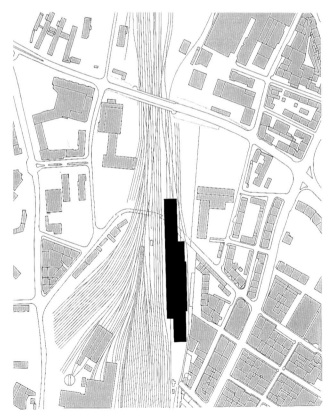

Exterior view of the annex service building (this page and opposite top and bottom). The plan shows the five railway tracks running over inspection pits along the total length of the building (perspectives and p. 108).

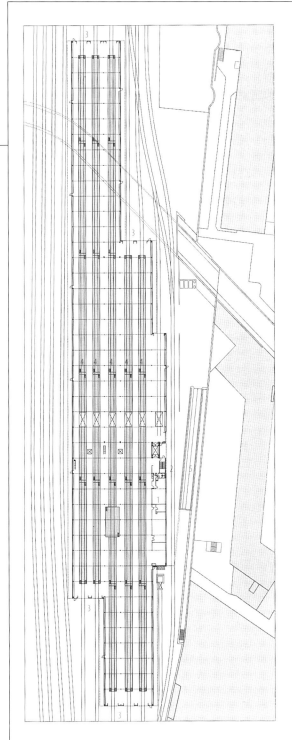

GROUND FLOOR PLAN

1. SERVICE ANNEX
2. STAFF ENTRANCE
3. TRAINS ENTRANCES
4. RAILWAY TRACKS
5. VEHICLES ACCESS

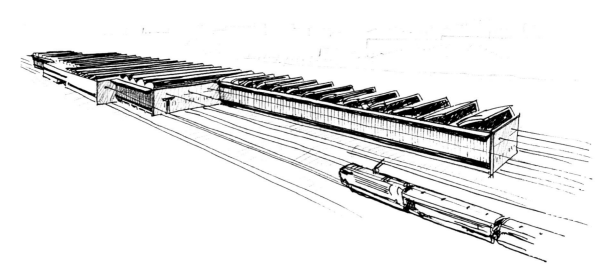

Views show the two distinct façade treatments, in wood for the main building's long walls and in aluminum for the annex service building and the main building's end walls with train entrances (this page and opposite). The main building's façade (overleaf)— with its shiny aluminum sheds and overhang—protects the rough-cut, dark, oversized shingles above a continuous strip window revealing the metal structure inside that is supported by a flattened exposed concrete base.

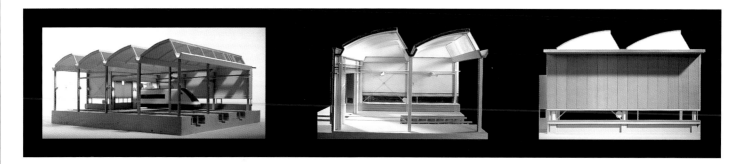

METAL FAÇADE ELEVATION

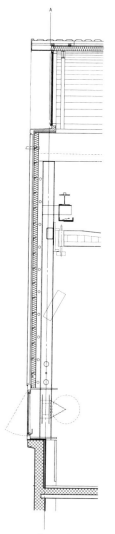

METAL FAÇADE SECTION

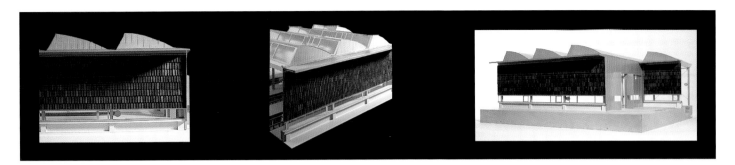

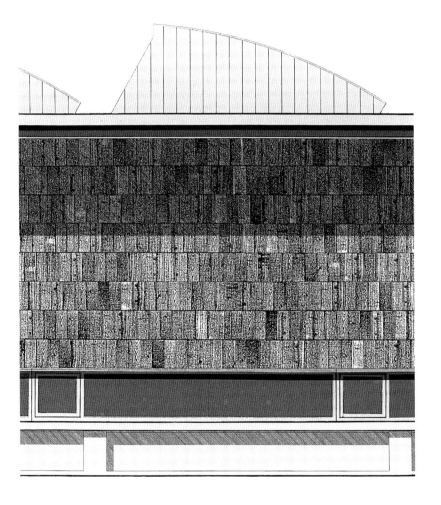

WOOD FAÇADE ELEVATION

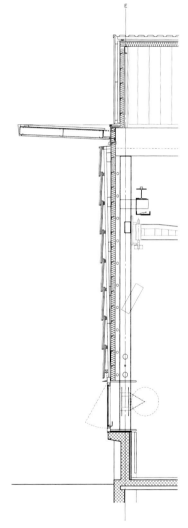

WOOD FAÇADE SECTION

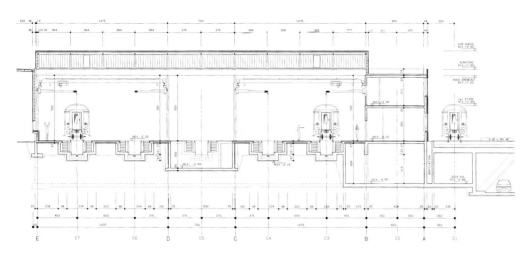

TRANSVERSAL SECTION

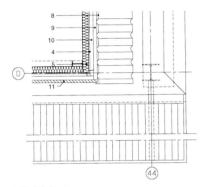

SHED LEVEL PLAN

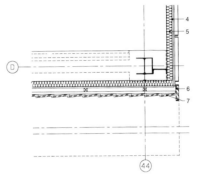

REVETMENT BOIS LEVEL PLAN

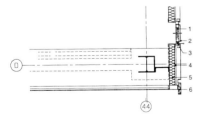

WINDOW LEVEL PLAN

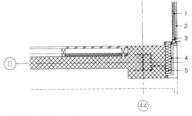

BASE/SOCLE LEVEL PLAN

CORNER DETAILS

1. THERMAL INSULATION
2. ANODIZED ALUMINUM SHEETING
3. INSULATING ALUMINUM PROFILE
4. INSULATION
5. INSULATION SUPPORT
6. ANODIZED ALUMINUM SHEETING ON PLYWOOD PANELS
7. PINE SHINGLES IMPREGNATED WITH GRAY COLOR
8. CORRUGATED STEEL SHEETING
9. GALVANISED Z PROFILE
10. WOOD BOARDING
11. FLAT STEEL SHEET PANELS

Metal-Stone ▶

EOS Headquarters

The head office for EOS (Energie Ouest Suisse SA) occupies a peaceful plot in the heart of Lausanne, in the shade of a majestic cedar tree. The building houses more than a hundred employees and provides seventy-three offices, conference rooms, lecture rooms, and a cafeteria. The archives, technical rooms, and parking for fifty-two vehicles are located in the basement levels. The steep slope of the site, which allows for only three levels aboveground at the back of the buildings, led to the creation of large internal light wells to allow for a maximum use of daylight and natural ventilation. The basic architectural concern was to make a single building in terms of function and image, starting from two distinct volumes of different heights imposed by the urban regulations. The façade's details search for this unity by suggesting the missing volume between the two blocks, therefore treating the internal lateral façades as sections, and by stressing the horizontality through the apron and the brise-soleils that appear as if they were detached from the façade. The fifth floor, obviously out of this horizontal continuity, is treated differently, almost as a joint between the main body and the roof.

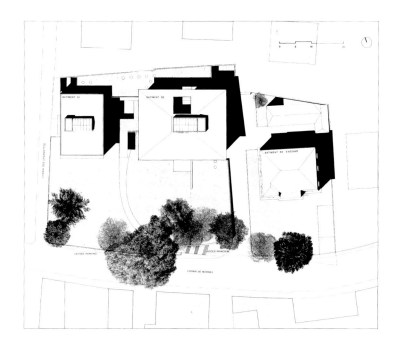

Harmoniously combining diverse materials, the main façade (this page) is treated in clear anodized aluminum for window frames and brise-soleils plus richly veined polished green granite for the spandrel panels. The internal side elevations (opposite) combine a lighter, sandblasted granite with larger clear anodized aluminum panels. Neutral exposed concrete completes the palette for the pillars and the roof structure.

SECTION THROUGH ENTRY

WEST ELEVATION

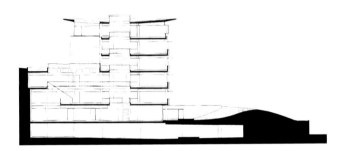

TRANSVERSAL SECTION

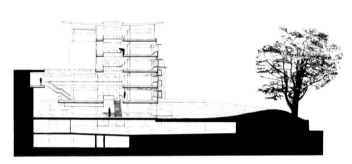

SECTION THROUGH LIGHT WELLS

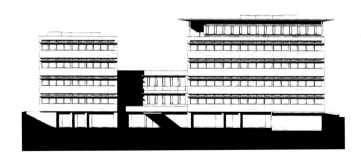

SOUTH ELEVATION

EAST ELEVATION

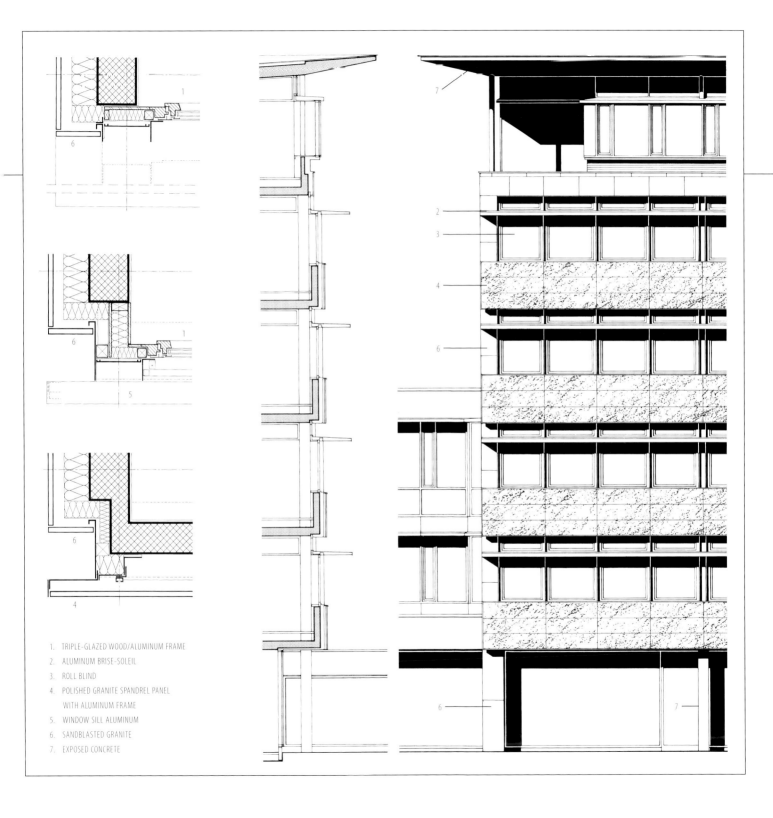

1. TRIPLE-GLAZED WOOD/ALUMINUM FRAME
2. ALUMINUM BRISE-SOLEIL
3. ROLL BLIND
4. POLISHED GRANITE SPANDREL PANEL
   WITH ALUMINUM FRAME
5. WINDOW SILL ALUMINUM
6. SANDBLASTED GRANITE
7. EXPOSED CONCRETE

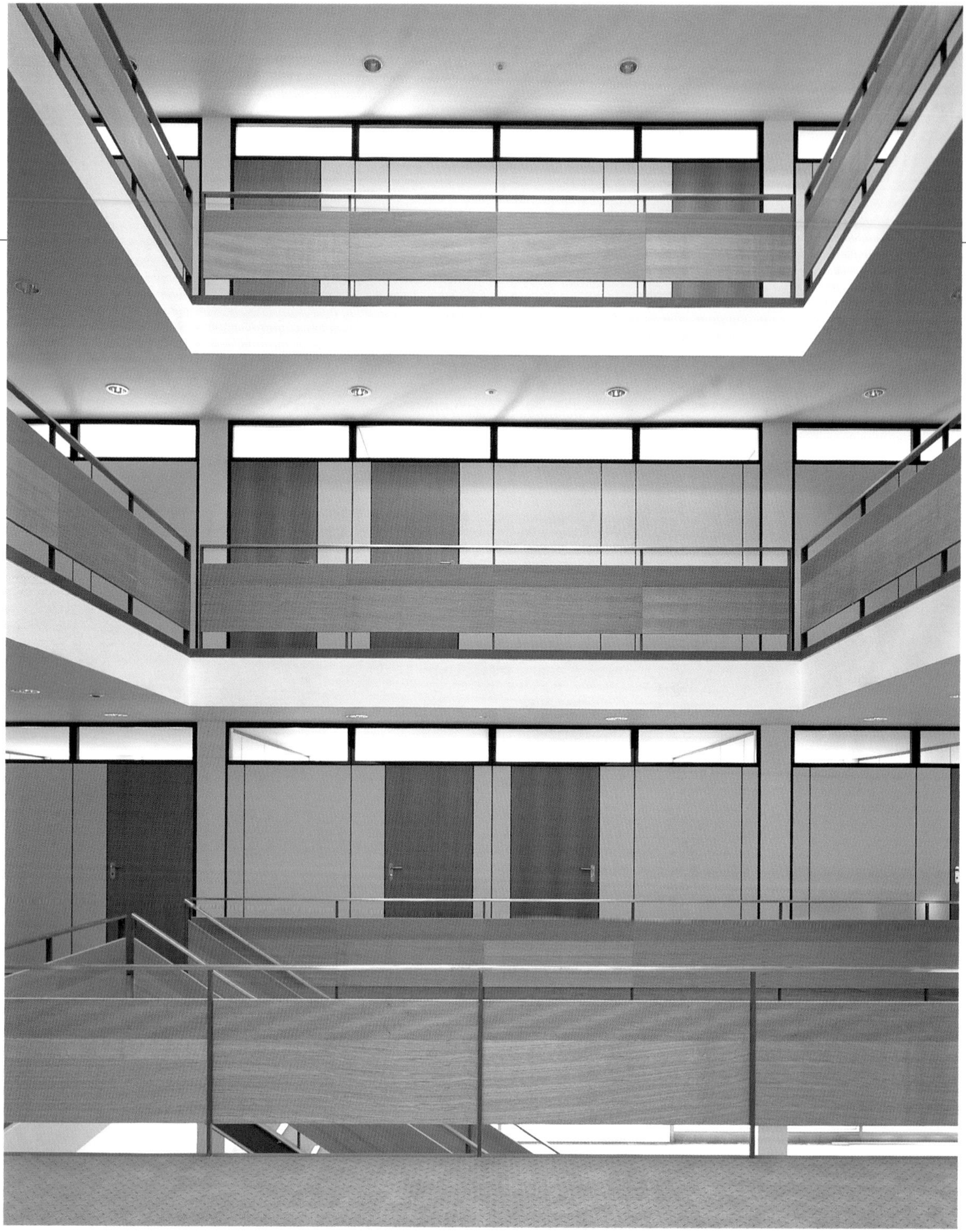

In the entrance hall and the main staircase (this page) leading to the first floor, the "piano nobile" around the central atrium space (opposite), the materials palette includes green polished granite on the floor at ground level as well as white plastered ceilings and columns and beechwood accenting the partitions, office doors, and balustrade.

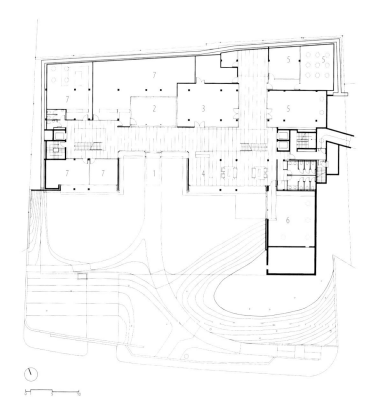

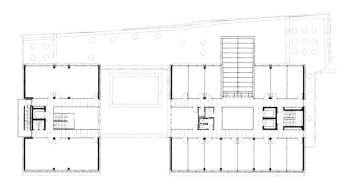

THIRD FLOOR PLAN

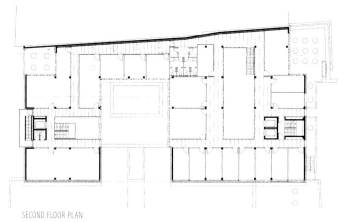

SECOND FLOOR PLAN

GROUND FLOOR PLAN

1. MAIN ENTRANCE
2. PATIO
3. CONFERENCE ROOM

4. RECEPTION ROOM
5. SEMINAR ROOM
6. CAFETERIA
7. OFFICE SPACE

Interior views show the strong presence of daylight and transparency arrived at via a series of skylights, atriums, and lateral openings.

Golay Buchel Headquarters

The new Golay Buchel headquarters is located at the west entrance of Lausanne, on the shores of Lake Geneva. The total forty-three thousand square feet (four thousand square meters) of floor space is distributed on four levels, each split in two parts that function independently. The first half is for Golay Buchel and the other one is to be leased. The building is inscribed in a simple volume that has been partially carved out. The resulting voids generate a series of spaces that separate these parts, creating a passage at the ground level for differentiated entrances and an atrium space around which the Golay Buchel offices are arranged. In turn the spatial complexity thus produced and the consequent permeability to natural light enrich the interior-exterior relationship. Two kinds of stones, a polished and a sandblasted granite, together with the anodized aluminum detailing, serve to articulate the base and the main body of the building.

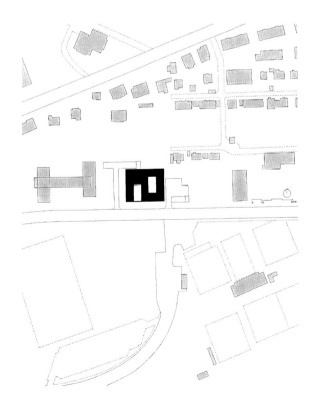

Views showing the rear façade from the north (top); the main façade on the south with its loggia on the first floor (middle and opposite); and the building as approached from the west (bottom).

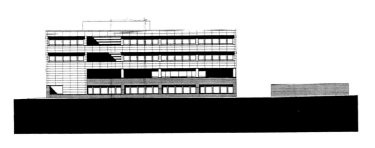

SOUTH ELEVATION

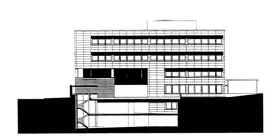

EAST ELEVATION

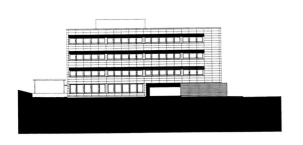

WEST ELEVATION

NORTH ELEVATION

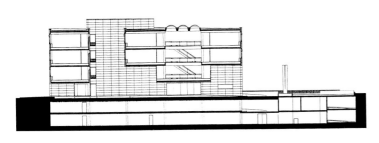

LONGITUDINAL SECTION BY PASSAGE

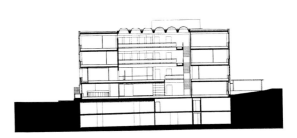

TRANSVERSAL SECTION BY CENTRAL SPACE

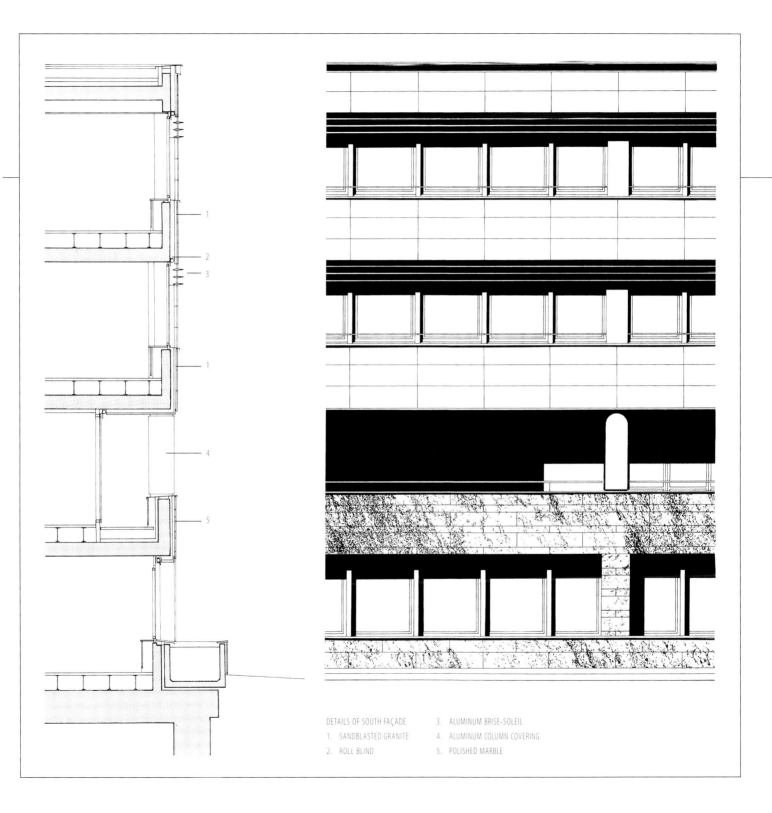

DETAILS OF SOUTH FAÇADE

1. SANDBLASTED GRANITE
2. ROLL BLIND
3. ALUMINUM BRISE-SOLEIL
4. ALUMINUM COLUMN COVERING
5. POLISHED MARBLE

Golay Buchel Headquarters

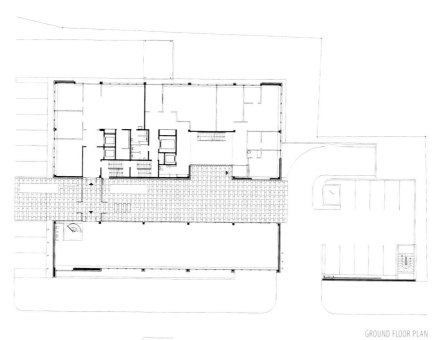

The intimacy of the internal outdoor space at ground floor level (opposite), created by carving out the overall volume, is noticeable in the composition of the ground and first floor plans.

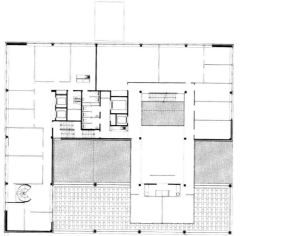

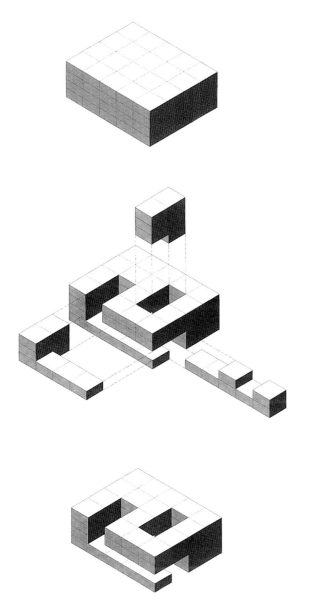

A drawing illustrates the spatial voids created by the subtraction of occupied mass (opposite) that creates a series of interconnecting outdoor spaces.

Although austere, the public interior spaces are relaxed and convivial due to the daylight filtered by the deep skylight and lateral openings and the balanced presence of beechwood and aluminum detailing, which is set off by the simple white plaster of the slabs, the pillars, and the skylight itself. Another view shows the entrance hall and the atrium space above it (opposite).

The atrium space (opposite) around
which the offices are organized houses
a two-story high acoustic panel by the
Swiss artist Jean-Luc Manz.

Nestlé Headquarters Renovation

The Nestlé Headquarters in Vevey is one of the most remarkable administrative buildings in the French-speaking part of Switzerland. Completed in 1960, this major work of the architect Jean Tschumi was extended in 1975 and has been the object of diverse transformations or additions. The obsolescence of the technical installations and the evolution of functional demands clearly mandated an integral renovation of Tschumi's building. The magnitude of this operation allowed for a wider revision of the project, which in turn resulted in the proposal for a new element to link the two buildings and thus enhance the unity and coherence of the whole. This intervention on a modern building (one listed in the Historical Monuments inventory) poses new questions, particularly about the strategies of approach and the choice of means for intervention, in a complex situation combining different degrees of action such as the restoration, the transformation, and the creation of new elements.

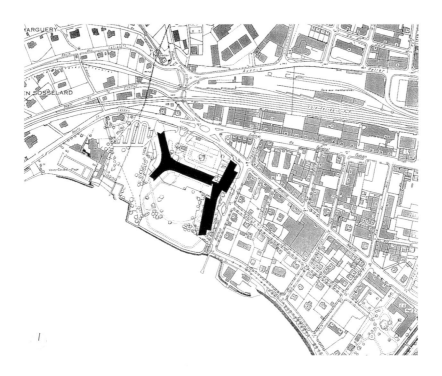

NESTLE HEADQUARTERS
RENOVATION 1997–2000

SIXTH FLOOR
NEW SKYLIGHT OVER CHAMBORD STAIRCASE SPACE

NEW TASTING CENTER AND PRODUCTS EXHIBITION

NEW BELVEDERE HALL

NEW LIAISON SPACE BETWEEN A AND B BUILDINGS

FIFTH FLOOR
NEW STAIRCASE GENERAL MANAGEMENT

FIFTH TO FIRST FLOOR
NEW OFFICE SPACES

GROUND FLOOR
NEW ENTRANCE HALL EXTENSION AND VISITORS' CENTER

BUILDING A
JEAN TSCHUMI, 1960
ENTIRELY RENOVATED

BUILDING B
BURCKHARDT & PARTNER, 1975
SIXTH FLOOR AND
LIAISON SPACE RENOVATION

  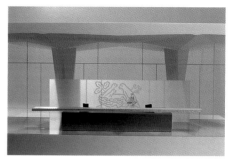

DETAIL NEW FAÇADE

1. ANODIZED ALUMINUM PANEL
2. ANODIZED "GRINATAL" ALUMINUM PANEL
3. ANODIZED ALUMINUM SHEET COVERING STEEL MULLION
4. ANODIZED EXTRUDED ALUMINUM BRISE-SOLEIL
5. ANODIZED EXTRUDED ALUMINUM WINDOW FRAME
    TRIPLE GLAZING WITH VENETIAN BLIND INCLUDED
6. ALUMINUM GRILL
7. ACCES FLOOR
8. EXISTING SCREEN ON SLAB
9. VENTILATION DUCT
10. SUSPENDED COLD CEILING ALUMINUM WITH POWDER COAT FINISH

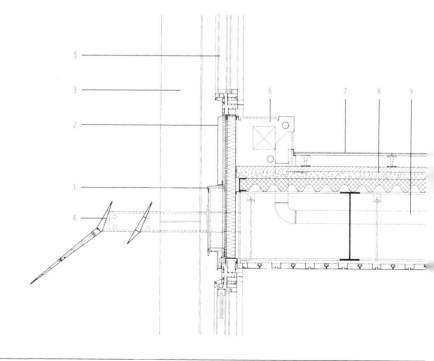

SECTION THROUGH SOUTH ELEVATION

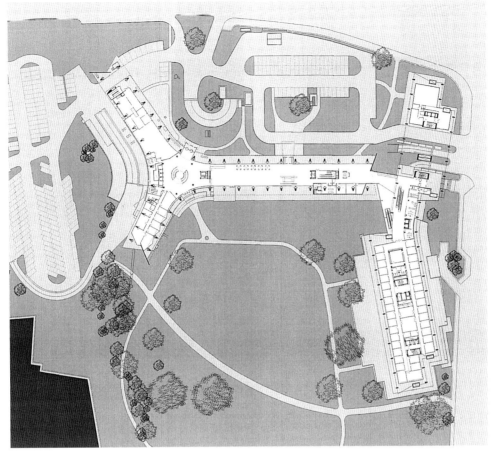

GROUND FLOOR PLAN

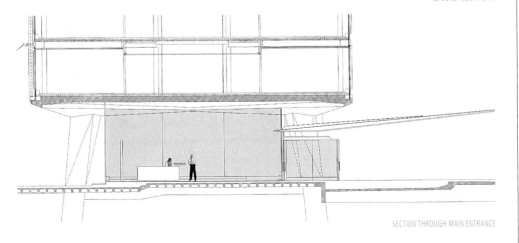

SECTION THROUGH MAIN ENTRANCE

The original Jean Tschumi façades were completely rebuilt with modern technology but maintain their original aesthetics (opposite). At ground level, the project manages to reorganize the connection between the two buildings while reinforcing the notion of transparency towards the lake and extending the original hall to the east.

While maintaining the original corridor and cellular office configuration, the whole mass was rebuilt with new furniture and partitions designed to achieve flexibility and transparency and increase teamwork and meeting spaces. The top floors, including the belvedere (top), were redesigned to host different public functions.

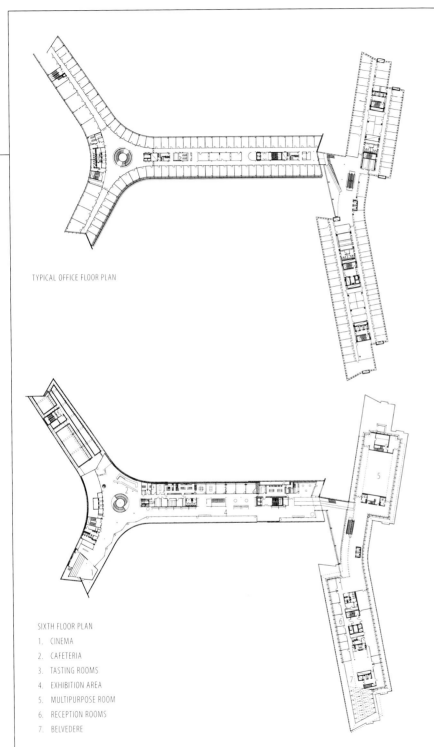

TYPICAL OFFICE FLOOR PLAN

SIXTH FLOOR PLAN
1. CINEMA
2. CAFETERIA
3. TASTING ROOMS
4. EXHIBITION AREA
5. MULTIPURPOSE ROOM
6. RECEPTION ROOMS
7. BELVEDERE

EXISTING VIEW

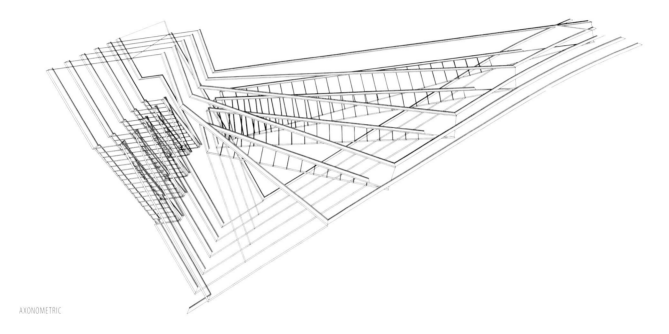

AXONOMETRIC

EXISTING LIAISON ELEMENT

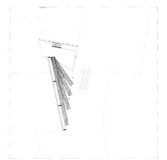

NEW LIAISON SPACE—SCHEME

NEW LIAISON SPACE—FIFTH FLOOR

The new liaison space is intended
to enhance the unity and coherence
of the center, connecting the two
buildings through a completely
glazed six-level-high space. The
concept evolved from a series of
ramps, which vary in length and
slope. The originals varied in length
but not in slope, in order to link the
two buildings–whose different slabs
varied in level on every floor.

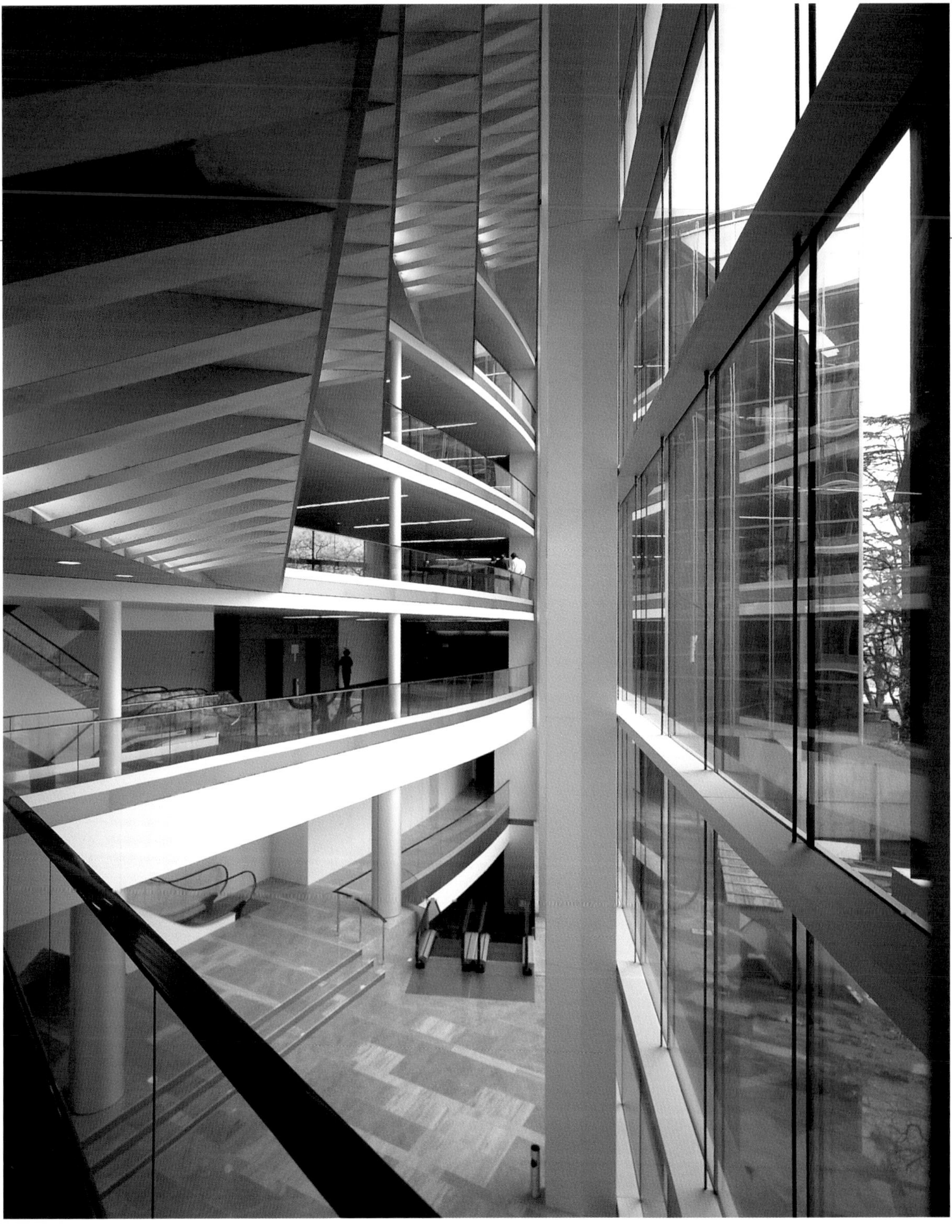

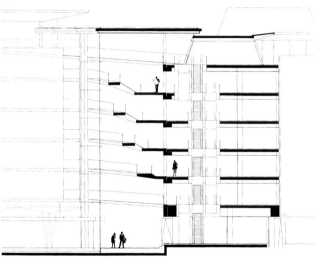

TRANSVERSAL SECTION OF NEW LIAISON SPACE

Views of the new liaison space, from the first floor (opposite), from the fifth floor (top), and on the fourth floor (bottom). The new staircase links the general management on the fifth floor with the product exhibition area on the top level (following page).

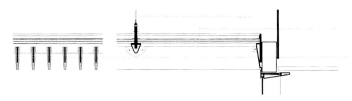

1. Cuspente acier peinte en blanc
2. Verre feuilleté 2 X 8 mm PVB translucide

3. Lamelle bois érable massif

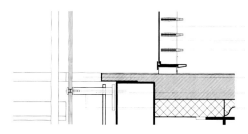

4. Montants acier + carrossage tôle aluminium eloxé naturel é
5. Verre PYROSWISS ép: 8 mm R30
3. Lamelle bois érable massif

6. Arrêt de chape acier inox
7. Console acier Ø 40
8. Carrossage acier inox Ø 44

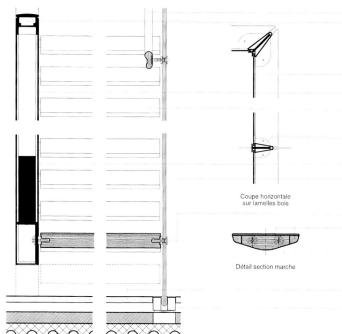

9. Profil main-courante bois wengé massif
10. Profil aluminium extrudé eloxé naturel

5. Verre PYROSWISS ép: 8 mm R30

11. Tôle aluminium ép: 4 mm
eloxé naturel collé sur sous-construction acier
12. Marche bois wengé massif + multi-plis

13. Acier carrossé aluminium eloxé naturel ép: 2 mm

14. Limon acier 300 X 100

15. Lame de verre trempé 292 X 4600 X 19 mm

Coupe horizontale
sur lamelles bois

16. Douilles à épaulement + vis acier inox de décolletage
17. Bois Wengé massif

18. Multi-plis

Détail section marche

19. Faux-plancher + moquette

20. Guidage du verre sans appuis

Appendix ▶

List of Works and Credits

HOUSE IN TORTUGUITAS
Tortuguitas, Provincia de Buenos Aires, Argentina 1987
Clients: Ignacio and Celina Dahl Rocha
Project Author: Billoch–Dahl Rocha–Ramos, Architects
Project Team: Ignacio Dahl Rocha with Francisco Billoch and Juan Ignacio Ramos
Awards: Biennale of Buenos Aires 1989
Photographers: Roberto Riverti, Ignacio Dahl Rocha

HOUSE IN SAN ISIDRO
San Isidro, Provincia de Buenos Aires, Argentina 1988
Clients: Christian and Claudia Schmiegelow
Project Author: Billoch–Dahl Rocha–Ramos, Architects
Project Team: Francisco Billoch, Ignacio Dahl Rocha, and Juan Ignacio Ramos
Awards: 1988, Finalist Palladio Prize, Vicenza, Italy,
1989, Biennale de Buenos Aires, Argentina
Structural Engineer: Miguel Durlach
Contractor: Madero and Lenhardson
Photographer: Roberto Riverti

HOUSE IN LUTRY
Lutry, Vaud, Switzerland 1984–1986
Clients: Denise and Urs von Stockar
Project Author: Richter et Gut SA
Architect Team: Jacques Richter, Bernard Emonet
Structural Engineer: Giacomini et Jolliet SA
Landscape Architect: Stephen Seymour
Photographers: Jacques Richter, Yves André

ESPACITE
La Chaux de Fonds, Neuchâtel, Switzerland 1987–1995
Client: SUVA, Caisse Nationale d'Assurances,
CPEN, Caisse Pensions Etat Neuchâtel
CPCF, Caisse Pensions Ville de la Chaux-de-Fonds
Architect Team: Jacques Richter, Ignacio Dahl Rocha, Kenneth Ross, Bernard Emonet, Alcibiades Manias, Carine Lombardi, Stéphane Kury, Barry Stanton, Gareth Pierce
Civil Engineer: GIESP—Groupement d'ingénieurs civils
Structural Engineer: Jean-Henri Petignat
Electrical Engineer: Scherler SA—Ingénieurs conseils
Mechanical Engineer: Bureau Planair SA
Sanitary Engineer: Laurent Geiser SA
Constructor: SD—Société Générale de Construction SA
Photographer: Yves André

FAE CONTEMPORARY ART MUSEUM
Pully, Vaud, Switzerland 1990–1991
Client: FAE—Fondation Asher B. Edelman
Architect Team: Jacques Richter, Ignacio Dahl Rocha, Christian Motte, Cecilia Carena
Structural Engineer: François Bapst
Mechanical Engineer: Etudes Génie Climatique SA
Electrical Engineer: Betelec SA
Lighting Consultant: Rick Shaver
Photographer: Pierre Boss

HOUSING BUILDING IN PRILLY
Prilly, Vaud, Switzerland 1991–1995
Client: Caisse de Pension de La Banque Cantonale Vaudoise
Project Team: Jacques Richter, Ignacio Dahl Rocha, Kenneth Ross, Manuel Perez
Civil Engineer: Moned Pigvet + Associés, Janin et Girard SA
Contractor: Bernard Nicod SA
Photographer: Yves André

SWHOME HOUSING CONCEPT
1992–1994
Architect Team: Jacques Richter, Ignacio Dahl Rocha, Salomé Grisard, Alcibiades Manias, Gilles Richter
Consultant: Göhner Merkur SA
Photographer: Pierre Boss
Models: Yves Gigon

HOUSES IN CHAILLY
Lausanne, Vaud, Switzerland 1995–1996
Clients: P. et C. Wiesel—C. et E. Felley
Architect Team: Jacques Richter, Ignacio Dahl Rocha, Manuela Toscan, Bernard Emonet, Olivier Bottarelli
Structural Engineer: Tibère Wiesel
Photographer: Yves André
Model: René Jeanneret

FOREST REFUGE
Vallée de Joux, Vaud, Switzerland 1993–1995
Client: Service Cantonal des Forêts
Architect Team: Jacques Richter, Ignacio Dahl Rocha, Kenneth Ross
Contractor: Entreprise E. Berney SA, Le Brassus
Photographers: Ignacio Dahl Rocha, Yves André
Models: Aurel Aebi, Patrick Reymond

SCHOOL OF AGRICULTURE IN GRANGE VERNEY
Moudon, Vaud, Switzerland 1990
Client: Service cantonal d'agriculture
Architect Team: Jacques Richter, Ignacio Dahl Rocha
Photographer: Yves André
Models: Marc Menoud

JUMBO SHOPPING MALL
Villars-sur-Glâne, Fribourg, Switzerland 1991–1995
Client: Centre Commercial Moncor SA, Maus Frères SA
Architect Team: Jacques Richter, Ignacio Dahl Rocha, Christian Leibbrandt, Kenneth Ross, Bruno Tschudi, Michel Paganin, Didier Grisoni, Patrick Gaberell, Renaud Giroud
Associate Architect: J.-P. Gillard + Associés (Direction des travaux)
Structural Engineer: Baeriswyl et Wicht SA
Electrical Engineer: Mottier SA
Mechanical Engineer: Intertecnic SA
Photographer: Yves André

TRAIN MAINTENANCE BUILDING
Genèva, Genèva, Switzerland 1995–1999
Client: CFF, Chemin de Fers Fédéraux
Project Group: AIAG—Association d'ingénieurs et d'architectes pour la Gare de Genèva
Architect Team: Jacques Richter, Ignacio Dahl Rocha, Kenneth Ross, Michel Paganin, Stéphanie Bender, Alain Jaquenod, Christian Gonin, Gilles Richter
Civil Engineer: H. Frey SA
Structural Engineer: Moncef Boubaker SA
Infrastructure Engineer: De Cérenville Géotechnique SA
Mechanical Engineer: Chammartin et Spicher SA
Electrical Engineer: M. Hurni et L. Richard
Photographer: Yves André
Models: Yves Gigon

EOS HEADQUARTERS
Lausanne, Vaud, Switzerland 1991–1995
Client: EOS SA, Energie de l'Ouest-Suisse SA
Architect Team: Jacques Richter, Ignacio Dahl Rocha, Kenneth Ross, Bernard Emonet, Carine Lombardi, Olivier Bottarelli, Stéphane Kury
Civil Engineer: Stucky Ingénieurs Conseils SA
Infrastructure Engineer: De Cérenville Géotechnique SA
Metal Engineer: Jean-Henri Petignat
Energy Concept: Sorane SA
Mechanical Engineer: Pierre Chuard SA
Electrical Engineer: Betelec SA
Photographer: Yves André
Models: Marc Menoud

GOLAY BUCHEL HEADQUARTERS
Lausanne, Vaud, Switzerland 1992–1997
Client: Golay Buchel & Cie SA
Architect Team: Jacques Richter, Ignacio Dahl Rocha, Kenneth Ross, Manuel Perez, Carine Lombardi, Didier Grisoni
Structural Engineer: Marmier et Hunziker SA
Mechanical Engineer: Etudes Génie Climatique SA
Electrical Engineer: Betelec SA
Landscape Architect: Stephen Seymour
Contractor: Geilinger SA
Photographer: Yves André
Models: Marc Menoud

NESTLE HEADQUARTERS RENOVATION
Vevey, Vaud, Switzerland 1996–2000
Client: Nestlé
Project Group: Consortium Bergère 2000
Architect Team: Jacques Richter, Ignacio Dahl Rocha, Kenneth Ross, Christian Leibbrandt, Manuel Perez, Bernard Emonet, Daniel Hernandez, Diego Behrend, Eduardo Hunziker, Olivier Lyon, Mathieu Thibault, Carine Lombardi, Salvatore Mercuri, Patricia Leal Laredo, Cédric Simon, Emanuel Oesch, Gilles Richter, Stéphanie Bender, Philippe Trim, Philippe Beboux, Barbara Moyano, Bruno Emmer, Pierre Jaquier
Structural Engineer: Tappy Bornand Michaud SA
Electrical Engineer: Amstein et Walthert SA
Mechanical Engineer: Jakob Forrer SA
Sanitary Engineer: Hermann Schumacher SA
Project Management: Steiner Engineering SA
Landscape Architect: Christophe Hüsler
Photographers: Nestec SA, Yves André Mario Carrieri
Models: Yves Gigon

ACKNOWLEDGMENTS

To our clients for their trust and respect.

To our associates, Kenneth Ross and Christian Leibbrandt, for their precious contribution and to the rest of the staff for their generous commitment.

To Max Richter and the departed Marcel Gut for having preceded us.

To Pancho Liernur and Jacques Gubler for their appreciation and recognition of our work.

To Oscar Riera Ojeda and Rockport Publishers for this book and to Patricia Leal Laredo and Caroline Dionne for their help in putting it together.

Dedicated to Chantal and Celina.